OECD
ECONOMIC
SURVEYS

1993-1994

NORWAY

ORGANISATION FOR ECONOMIC CO-OPERATION AND DEVELOPMENT

ORGANISATION FOR ECONOMIC CO-OPERATION AND DEVELOPMENT

Pursuant to Article 1 of the Convention signed in Paris on 14th December 1960, and which came into force on 30th September 1961, the Organisation for Economic Co-operation and Development (OECD) shall promote policies designed:

— to achieve the highest sustainable economic growth and employment and a rising standard of living in Member countries, while maintaining financial stability, and thus to contribute to the development of the world economy;
— to contribute to sound economic expansion in Member as well as non-member countries in the process of economic development; and
— to contribute to the expansion of world trade on a multilateral, non-discriminatory basis in accordance with international obligations.

The original Member countries of the OECD are Austria, Belgium, Canada, Denmark, France, Germany, Greece, Iceland, Ireland, Italy, Luxembourg, the Netherlands, Norway, Portugal, Spain, Sweden, Switzerland, Turkey, the United Kingdom and the United States. The following countries became Members subsequently through accession at the dates indicated hereafter: Japan (28th April 1964), Finland (28th January 1969), Australia (7th June 1971) and New Zealand (29th May 1973). The Commission of the European Communities takes part in the work of the OECD (Article 13 of the OECD Convention).

Publié également en français.

Table of contents

Introduction   9

I.   Recent developments and short-term prospects   11

A modest recovery   11
Main features of the upturn   11
Short-term outlook: a more broadly based recovery   26

II. Economic policies   29

Overview   29
Monetary management   29
The fiscal stance   38
Structural reform   46

III. The labour market: performance and scope for reform   53

Symptoms of rising structural unemployment   54
The role of institutions and policies   64
Prospects for reform   77

IV. Conclusions   80

Notes and references   85

Bibliography   89

Annex
Calendar of main economic events   91

Statistical annex   97

3

Tables

Text

1. Demand and output   13
2. Household appropriation account   16
3. Labour market developments   21
4. Prices, wages and costs   22
5. Short-term prospects   27
6. Banks' balance sheets   34
7. Sources of domestic credit expansion   37
8. Money growth   38
9. Government expenditure, revenue and net lending position   40
10. State budget balance: projections and outcomes   41
11. Agricultural support in Norway   49
12. Effects of agricultural reforms   50
13. Job finding, job losing and spell duration   60
14. Unemployment rates by educational attainment and sex, 1992   63
15. Changes in employment and participation rates   63
16. Expenditures on labour market programmes, 1992   67
17. Employment and labour force growth, pre and post the 1985-86 demand boom   70
18. Active labour market programmes   73

Statistical annex

Selected background statistics   98
A. Supply and use of resources   99
B. Gross domestic product by origin (current prices)   100
C. Gross domestic product by origin (volume)   101
D. General government income and expenditure   102
E. Labour market   103
F. Balance of payments   104
G. Foreign trade by area   105
H. Prices and wages   106
I. Money and credit   107
J. Production and employment structures   108

K.	Productivity and investment structure	109
L.	Labour-market indicators	110
M.	Public sector	111

Diagrams

Text

1.	Growth performance and its main determinants	12
2.	Oil and gas activities	14
3.	Progress in household financial consolidation	17
4.	Household demand	18
5.	Mainland business investment	20
6.	Inflation performance	23
7.	The current balance and its major components	25
8.	Net foreign debt and investment income	26
9.	Exchange rate behaviour and official reserves	31
10.	Interest rate developments	32
11.	Banking situation	35
12.	Bank lending	36
13.	State budget balance	39
14.	Public expenditure	44
15.	Fiscal sustainability	45
16.	Unemployment rates	54
17.	Labour force developments	55
18.	Distribution of employment	57
19.	Employment rates	58
20.	Alternative measures of labour utilisation	59
21.	Impact of frequency and duration on the unemployment rate	60
22.	Concentration of unemployment	62
23.	Wage developments	65
24.	Job finding probabilities	71
25.	Unemployed adjusted for effective labour supply	74

BASIC STATISTICS OF NORWAY

THE LAND

Area (1 000 sq. km), 1983	324	Major cities (1.1.93):	
Agricultural area (1 000 sq. km), 1983	9	Oslo	473 344
Productive forests (1 000 sq. km), 1983	65	Bergen	218 105

THE PEOPLE

Population (31.12.1992)	4 299 231	Civilian employment, 1992	1 970 000
Number of inhabitants per sq. km	13	*of which:*	
Net natural increase (average 1987-92)	13 624	Industry (%)	23.5
Per 1 000 inhabitants (average 1987-92)	3.2	Agriculture, forestry and fishing	5.6
		Other activities (%)	70.9

PRODUCTION

Gross domestic product, 1992		Gross fixed capital formation (1992):	
(NKr million)	701 650	Percentage of GDP	19.1
GDP per head (1992, US$)	26 321	Per head, US$	5 037

THE GOVERNMENT

Public consumption in 1992 (percentage of GDP)	22.4	Composition of Parliament (number of seats):	
General government current and capital		Labour Party	67
expenditure in 1992 (percentage of GDP)	57.5	Conservative Party	28
General government revenue in 1992		Christian Democratic Party	13
(percentage of GDP)	54.8	Centre (Agrarian) Party	32
		Progress Party	10
		Social Left Party	13
		Others	2
		Total	165
Last general elections: 1993		Next general elections: 1997	

FOREIGN TRADE

Exports of goods and services		Imports of goods and services	
(average 1987-92, as a % of GDP)	41.1	(average 1987-92, as a % of GDP)	36.9
of which:		Main imports in 1992 (percentage of total	
Gross freight and oil drilling (1987-92)	6.4	commodity imports):	
Main exports in 1992 (percentage of total		Ships	4.0
commodity exports):		Machinery, apparatus and transport	
Forestry products	3.4	equipment (excluding ships)	30.5
Base metals and products thereof	10.7	Raw materials (non-edible), including fuel	
Fish and fish products	6.6	and chemicals	12.4
Machinery, apparatus and transport		Base metals and products thereof	9.6
equipment (excluding ships)	7.9		

THE CURRENCY

Monetary unit: Krone		Currency units per US$, average of daily figures:	
		Year 1993	7.09
		December 1993	7.42

Note: An international comparison of certain basic statistics is given in an Annex table.

Introduction

Following several years of depressed output and employment, in the context of a sharp financial consolidation by households and firms and severe difficulties in the banking sector, there have been signs of recovery in Norway's Mainland economy over 1992-93. The emerging upturn has been slow, however, relying mainly on rising oil investment and public expenditure. On the other hand, with consumer confidence poor and business investment sluggish, private demand has remained weak until very recently. At the same time, the rate of inflation has stabilised at a low level and external cost competitiveness improved. With rising oil and gas revenues, the external current account has shown sizeable surpluses, leading to a rapid reduction in net foreign indebtedness.

Real growth is projected to gather momentum throughout 1994 and 1995, as – with financial consolidation apparently coming to an end – private expenditure is expected to respond positively to the easing of monetary conditions. In addition, the projected pick-up of world trade should provide impetus to the upturn. Unemployment should decline only marginally, as some cyclical recovery is expected in labour-force participation rates. With the continued slack in product and labour markets, inflation is expected to remain moderate. As oil and gas production should continue to expand rapidly, the current account surplus is projected to widen markedly.

Monetary conditions have eased considerably since external developments necessitated a shift to a floating exchange rate regime in late 1992. While the krone has remained broadly stable after a limited initial depreciation, short-term interest rates have progressively declined to below the levels recorded elsewhere in Europe. This has contributed to a marked improvement in bank profitability. Given the continued good inflation performance, long-term rates have also eased, suggesting enhanced monetary policy credibility. By contrast, budget consolidation has been lagging, as fiscal policy remained expansionary in 1993. While the

1994 Budget calls for a tightening of the fiscal stance, medium-term projections imply a continued rundown of the Government's net financial asset position over the medium term, despite increased oil revenue. On the structural side, greater emphasis has been put on the necessity to improve the functioning of the labour market in order to reduce unemployment.

Part I of the Survey briefly reviews recent trends and short-term prospects. Macroeconomic and structural policies are discussed in Part II. Part III examines in some detail Norway's labour-market performance with a view to identifying structural deficiencies and policy requirements in this area. Conclusions are presented in Part IV.

I. Recent developments and short-term prospects

A modest recovery

Although overall economic growth in Norway has strengthened since the beginning of the 1990s, it was not before early 1992 that Mainland GDP resumed its upward trend after several years of falling or stagnating output (Diagram 1). So far, the recovery has been slow by historical standards: while growth rates in the initial phase of previous cyclical upturns were typically in the 3 to 4 per cent range, Mainland GDP rose by only 2 per cent in 1992 and even weakened in the first half of 1993. However, the pause in growth in 1993 was to a large extent due to special factors (see below), which masked the underlying upward trend in economic activity. Most recent indicators point to a resumption of Mainland growth since the summer of 1993, as evidenced by the revival of consumer spending on durables and housing starts following the substantial easing of monetary conditions.

Main features of the upturn

The recovery has been driven largely by two impulses: an acceleration of offshore oil investments and continuous strong real growth in public expenditures, in particular in 1992. Indeed, in the early stages of the upturn, the public sector accounted for more than half of Mainland growth, while the rapid expansion of oil production, and hence exports, led to growth rates of total GDP that exceeded those of the Mainland economy by 1 to 2 percentage points (Table 1). By contrast, the growth contribution from the private non-energy sector has been minor, as reflected in the sluggishness of non-oil business investment and the relatively weak growth of "traditional" exports (despite recent gains in cost competitiveness).

11

Diagram 1. GROWTH PERFORMANCE AND ITS MAIN DETERMINANTS
Constant 1985 prices, seasonally adjusted

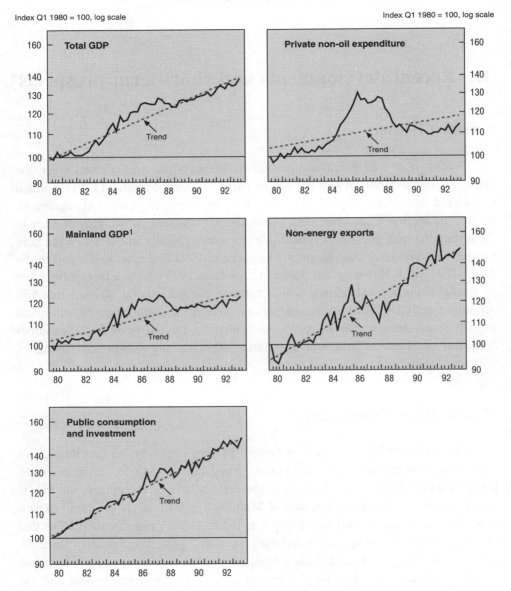

1. Excluding North Sea production, oil platforms and ships.
Sources: Norwegian Central Bureau of Statistics; OECD.

Table 1. **Demand and output**

Percentage changes from previous year, volumes (preceding year's prices)

	NKr million in 1987	1988	1989	1990	1991	1992	1993 H1[5]
Private consumption	298 054	−2.8	−2.8	2.8	0.0	1.8	1.2
Government consumption	116 044	0.5	2.6	2.1	2.6	4.6	1.8
Gross fixed capital formation[1]	157 395	0.2	−7.2	−14.5	−2.0	−1.4	17.4
of which:							
Residential construction	29 388	−3.8	−17.0	−17.1	−27.3	−15.9	−7.4
Oil sector[1]	91 935	−11.0	8.7	−12.7	31.0	8.5	37.1
Other business sector	78 149	−10.6	−21.6	−5.1	−5.9	4.6	−0.5
Government[2]	20 088	7.4	0.7	−7.1	14.4	2.4	8.9[4]
Stockbuilding[3]	1 190	−1.8	0.0	1.0	−0.6	−0.2	−0.5
Total domestic demand	572 683	−3.1	−2.9	−1.0	−0.5	1.5	−0.4
Exports of goods and services	200 224	5.5	10.7	8.1	6.1	6.1	0.2
of which:							
Exports of oil and gas	53 620	11.5	24.7	1.8	17.0	10.8	2.8
Imports of goods and services	211 427	−1.7	0.9	2.2	1.7	2.2	4.4
GDP	561 480	−0.5	0.6	1.7	1.6	3.3	1.4
Memorandum items:							
Mainland GDP	495 187	−1.7	−2.2	1.1	−0.6	2.0	1.3
OECD Europe GDP		3.9	3.3	3.0	1.1	1.1	−0.2

1. Including platforms under construction.
2. Excluding public enterprises.
3. Contribution to GDP growth, excluding platforms under construction.
4. Growth rates for other business sector and government investment in 1992 are heavily affected by adminstrative changes which occurred in the ownership structure of buildings used by the State.
5. First three quarters of 1993, seasonally adjusted and on an annual level, compared with the whole of 1992.
Source: OECD.

Boost from the oil sector

Investment in the oil sector has been buoyant in recent years (Table 1). It is expected to peak in the autumn of 1993, bringing its level for the year as a whole up to around 7½ percent of GDP from 6.3 per cent in 1992 (Diagram 2, panel A).[1] Such sharply rising oil investment has not only boosted overall capital formation – it now accounts for about one-third of total investment in Norway – but has also contributed significantly to Mainland growth, as oil equipment goods – production platforms in particular – are for a large part manufactured by

Diagram 2. **OIL AND GAS ACTIVITIES**

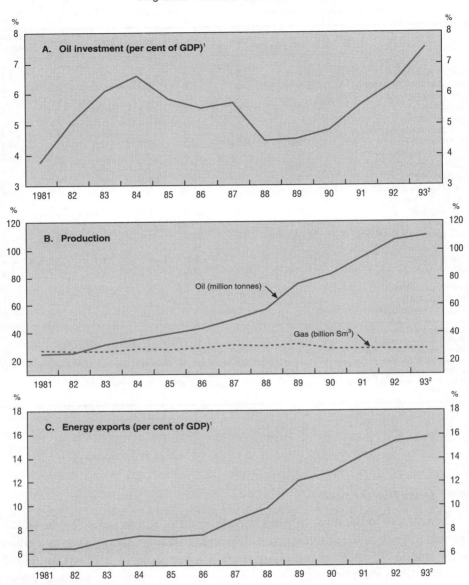

A. **Oil investment (per cent of GDP)**[1]

B. **Production**

Oil (million tonnes)

Gas (billion Sm³)

C. **Energy exports (per cent of GDP)**[1]

1. Constant 1993 prices.
2. OECD Secretariat estimates.
Sources: Norwegian Ministry of Finance; *National Accounts.*

14

Norwegian industry. On the basis of official estimates of the shares of domestic sourcing, the increases in oil investment may have added about 0.4 and 0.8 per cent to Mainland GDP in 1992 and 1993, respectively. Moreover, with expanding output capacity, energy exports – accounting for more than one-third of total exports – increased at double-digit rates in 1991-92, thus boosting overall economic growth (Diagram 2, panels B and C). After a temporary slowdown in late 1992 and early 1993, due mainly to difficult weather conditions, exports of raw oil and natural gas progressed by an additional 8 per cent in volume in the second quarter of 1993 compared with the same period of 1992.

Rising public expenditure

In recent years public consumption and investment were the main contributors to growth in the Mainland economy. Real public spending on goods and services grew by 4.2 per cent in 1992 and, despite reduced military equipment purchases and the completion of large investment projects, it is expected to expand by a further 1½ percent in 1993. This is, however, well below average growth rates of 3-4 per cent in the period 1987-1992. On the basis of latest official projections, Government consumption is likely to rise by 3 per cent in 1993 as a whole (see fiscal policy section below). Total public investment – even adjusted for the effects of administrative changes[2] – is expected to fall by more than 5 per cent in 1993, reflecting the termination of construction work for the Winter Olympics.

Slight improvement in household demand

Reflecting the expansionary fiscal policies pursued during 1990-92, rising public transfers and tax reliefs consistently accounted for more than half of the growth in households' real disposable income during that period (Table 2). The tax cuts implemented in 1992, in the context of an overall tax reform,[3] boosted incomes by 1¼ percentage points, while net public transfers added an additional 1¾ points. On present estimates, 1993 will be the first year since the mid-1980s when private sources account for the bulk of the total rise in households' real disposable income.

These developments have been reflected only partly in higher spending, as financial consolidation by households persisted in 1992 and into 1993. Following a further sharp rise in 1992, the household saving ratio edged up in the first half

15

Table 2. **Household appropriation account**

Percentage change from previous year

	1990	1991	1992	1993 [1]
Real consumption expenditure	2.8	0.0	1.8	1.7
Real disposable income	2.7	1.7	4.3	2.1
Contribution from:				
Wages	−0.7	0.2	0.7	0.4
Profit income	1.2	−0.4	0.1	0.7
Net public transfers	1.7	2.0	1.7	1.1
Net interest payments, etc.	0.4	0.0	1.2	1.1
Direct taxes [2]	0.2	0.0	0.7	−1.2
Saving ratio, level in percent	0.9	2.6	5.0	5.4
Memorandum item:				
Private consumption deflator	4.8	4.1	2.6	2.3

1. OECD Secretariat estimates, based on developments up to September/October.
2. A positive contribution implies that *real* direct taxes have been reduced. Does not include changes in social security taxes paid by employers.
Source: Norwegian Central Bureau of Statistics.

of 1993 and, at around 5-5$\frac{1}{2}$ per cent of disposable income, is now broadly back to the level of the early 1980s (Diagram 3, panel A). With households' fixed investment declining dramatically (Table 1), their net financial assets in relation to disposable income rose from 13 per cent in 1988 to 28 per cent by the end of 1992 and now probably exceed 30 per cent. Such continued attempts by households to consolidate their financial position may reflect the high real after-tax interest rates and low asset prices still prevailing until recently.

The effects of this financial consolidation process have been particularly evident in demand for housing and consumer durables. In early 1993, housing starts and purchases of cars and other durables were still below the levels recorded in the early 1980s (Diagram 4). The evolution of private consumption in the first half of 1993 was adversely affected by the introduction of the higher VAT rate from January 1993, which had led to a spending spree in late 1992 in anticipation of higher prices. As a result, consumer spending contracted in the first quarter of 1993, before rising in the second quarter. More recently, probably reflecting the easing in monetary conditions, household demand has picked up markedly. In August-October 1993, purchases of new cars were up 11 per cent from the same period of 1992, and housing starts grew by 17 per cent in the same

16

Diagram 3. **PROGRESS IN HOUSEHOLD FINANCIAL CONSOLIDATION**

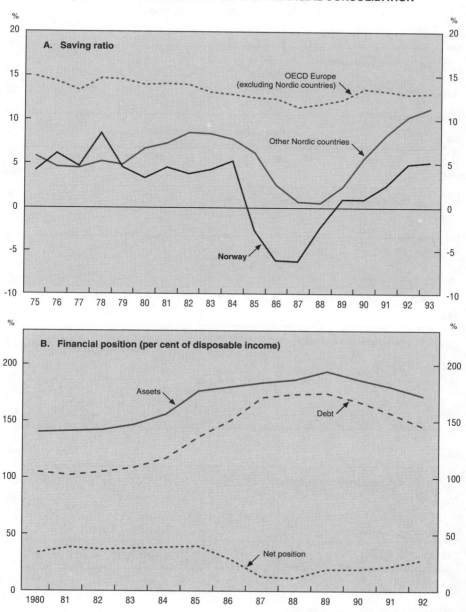

Sources: Bank of Norway; OECD, *National Accounts.*

17

Diagram 4. **HOUSEHOLD DEMAND**

Q1 1980 = 100, seasonally adjusted

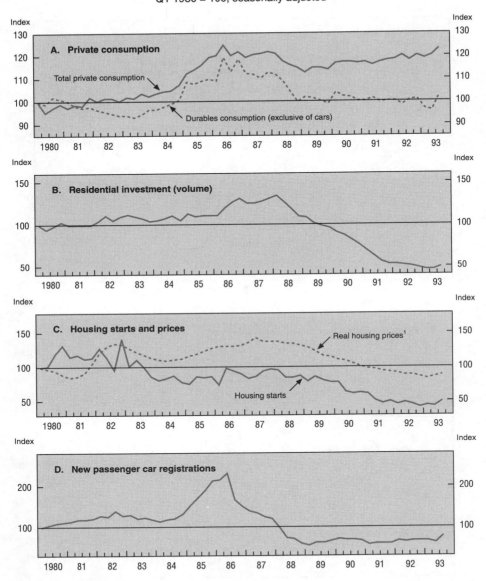

1. Deflated by the private consumption deflator.
Source: OECD, Quarterly *National Accounts, Main Economic Indicators.*

period. As well, in the second and third quarter of 1993, house prices rose for the first time since 1986, rebounding to their level of early 1992. This suggests that the decline in residential investment may be bottoming out.

Still sluggish (non-oil) business investment

The low growth rates of the Mainland economy since the boom years in the mid-1980s have led to markedly lower investment levels. While investment exceeded 20 per cent of value added in the Mainland business sector in 1986, this ratio declined to less than 15 per cent in 1992 and is likely to have recovered only slightly in 1993 (Diagram 5, panel A). Most of the reduction in business investment took place during the recession. Since then, the downward trend in Mainland investment has levelled off. Official estimates of capacity utilisation in the whole Mainland business sector indicate that, in recent years, production capacity, at least at an aggregate level, has been fully adequate given weak overall demand: in 1993, the capital/output ratio was still significantly above its trend level (Diagram 5, panel B). Although all branches have been affected, the fall in fixed capital formation has been particularly pronounced in service industries, such as wholesale and retail trade, which have been more exposed to the decline in domestic demand than manufacturing (Diagram 5, panels C and D).

As in the case of households, particularly high real interest rates reinforced the need for financial consolidation in the business sector. However, the recent easing of monetary conditions has substantially reduced financing costs and improved earnings among corporations. Moreover, the near doubling of share prices over the past year has boosted financial wealth, in particular of large enterprises. Given the wide fluctuations in capital spending, it is too early to say whether the modest pick-up in the midst of 1993 heralds a recovery in Mainland business investment, all the more so because latest investment intention surveys still indicate a fall in investment both this year and next.

Stabilising unemployment

Despite weak Mainland economic activity, the unemployment rate has remained stable at around 6 per cent (seasonally adjusted) since mid-1992 (Table 3), as active labour-market measures have been further expanded to cover about 3 per cent of the workforce. While the number of hours worked seems to have increased slightly over this period, the decline in total employment has

Diagram 5. **MAINLAND BUSINESS INVESTMENT**

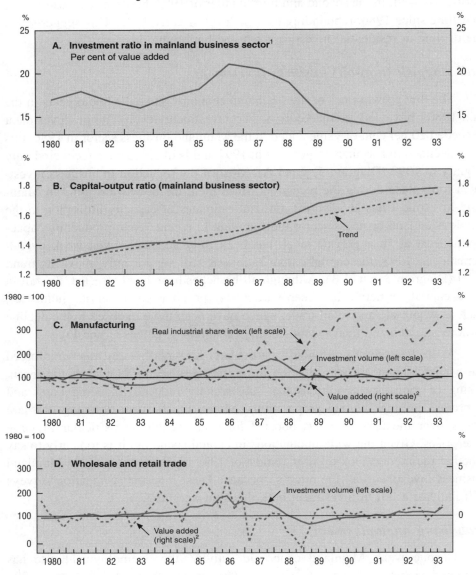

1. Excluding residential "sector", petroleum production and shipping. The figures are calculated as investment divided by value added in the sector.
2. Per cent change over 4 quarters, 3 quarters moving average.
Source: OECD, *National Accounts.*

Table 3. **Labour market developments**

	1989 Thousand persons	1990	1991	1992	1993[1]
		Per cent change from previous year			
Labour force	2 155	−0.6	−0.7	0.2	0.1
Employment, total	2 049	−0.9	−1.0	−0.3	−0.1
Public sector[2]	554	2.4	2.9	2.7	3.0
Private[2]	1 513	−2.0	−2.2	−1.5	−1.5
Unemployment	106	5.7	3.6	8.2	3.1
		As a percentage of the labour force			
Rate of unemployment[4]		5.2	5.5	5.9	6.2[3]

1. Growth from the third quarter of 1992 to the third quarter of 1993.
2. Annual figures based upon National Accounts, while 1993 figures are based upon Labour Market Surveys.
3. Third quarter, seasonally adjusted.
Source: Norwegian Central Bureau of Statistics, Labour Market Surveys.

bottomed out only very recently. Private-sector employment, though, has continued to contract, in particular in the service industries. The performance of the Norwegian labour market in recent years is more thoroughly discussed in Part III, the special chapter of this Survey.

Continued low inflation

After a long period of steady decline, inflation has broadly stabilised in the 2 to 2.5 per cent range since early 1992, with the consumer price index (CPI) up by 1.9 per cent over the 12 months to November 1993 (Diagram 6, panel A and Table 4). Further disinflation would probably have occurred in the absence of the increase in the VAT rate from January 1993, as the latter's effect on consumer prices was only partially offset by a general reduction in employers' social-security contributions (corresponding to approximately 2 per cent of the wage bill).[4] The depreciation of the Norwegian krone since its floating in December 1992, though relatively modest in trade-weighted terms (see below), has also contributed to stop the decline of consumer inflation. This is evident in the prices of imported consumer goods, which, contrary to the period from 1987 to 1992, grew more than the CPI in 1993 (Table 4). On the other hand, the decline in

21

Table 4. **Prices, wages and costs**

Percentage change from previous year

	1988	1989	1990	1991	1992	1993
Consumer prices	6.7	4.6	4.1	3.4	2.3	1.9[1]
Imported consumer goods	7.3	2.8	1.7	2.0	1.8	3.7[1]
Hourly wages in manufacturing	5.4	5.1	5.9	5.3	3.1	2.8[2]
Compensation per employee:						
Mainland economy	6.4	4.5	5.2	5.1	2.9	
Manufacturing	6.1	4.4	5.6	4.7	2.8	1.0[2]
Unit labour costs:						
Mainland economy	7.8	3.3	2.2	4.2	1.1	
Manufacturing	6.9	−0.5	2.5	3.8	1.1	-0.5[2]

1. November 1993/November 1992.
2. OECD Secretariat estimate.
Source: Norwegian Central Bureau of Statistics and OECD, *Main Economic Indicators.*

interest rates means that housing rentals are now increasing more slowly than the CPI (excluding food). As the disinflationary process has continued in competitor countries, the inflation differential in favour of Norway has been reduced from about 2 per cent in 1991 to about ½ percent by the autumn of 1993 (Diagram 6, panel B).

With persistently high unemployment and low inflation, wage growth has moderated substantially in recent years (Table 4). Settlements in the current wage round have been in the 2½ to 3 per cent range, unchanged from the preceding year. Given the cut in employers' social-security contributions noted above, however, the growth in labour costs slowed further in 1993. Thus, although the increase in labour productivity appears to be smaller than in previous years, unit labour costs have fallen somewhat. In combination with an estimated effective depreciation of the krone of around 3 per cent, this may have led to a 4-5 per cent decline in relative unit labour costs measured in common currency in 1993. While cost competitiveness has considerably improved in recent years (Diagram 6, panel C), absolute labour costs in Norway are nevertheless still high, exceeding the average level registered in trading partner countries by about 10 per cent.

Diagram 6. **INFLATION PERFORMANCE**

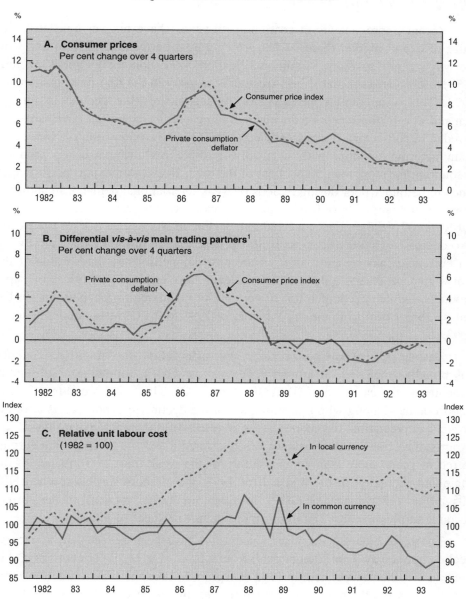

A. **Consumer prices**
Per cent change over 4 quarters

Consumer price index

Private consumption
deflator

B. **Differential *vis-à-vis* main trading partners**[1]
Per cent change over 4 quarters

Private consumption
deflator

Consumer price index

C. **Relative unit labour cost**
(1982 = 100)

In local currency

In common currency

1. Norway minus partners.
Source: OECD, *Main Economic Indicators, National Accounts.*

23

Rising external surplus

Recent improvements in cost competitiveness have not yet translated into gains of export market shares. After growing by 4 per cent in 1992 in line with Norway's export markets, "traditional" exports – *i.e.* non-energy goods, excluding also oil platforms and ships – rose only slightly in the first three quarters of 1993. This disappointing performance reflects mainly the decline in foreign demand due to the recession in major trading partner countries (Germany and Sweden in particular). It is also related to the specific composition of Norwegian manufacturing exports: with cyclically-sensitive raw-material-based products accounting for more than 50 per cent of the total, Norwegian export performance tends to be rather poor during periods of weak international demand. In addition, some special factors have been at play. Increased supply from Eastern Europe, in particular of metal products, has led to a decline in Norwegian market shares and also depressed export prices. As well, the depreciation of the Finnish and Swedish currencies has severely affected the cost competitiveness and profits of the Norwegian paper and pulp industry. Indeed, Norwegian export prices of paper products – which accounted for 10 per cent of manufacturing exports in 1991 – fell by 15 per cent from the third quarter of 1991 to the corresponding quarter in 1993.

Despite poor export performance, the trade deficit for "traditional" goods has broadly stabilised (at around 7 per cent of GDP), following a substantial widening in the early 1990s (Diagram 7, panel B). This reflects continued weak import demand along with a levelling off of the decline in export prices after the krone's depreciation. By contrast, as a result of the rapid expansion of oil exports, the offshore trade balance has registered a very large and rising surplus in recent years, more than compensating for the weak trade performance of the Mainland economy. In the first half of 1993, the offshore surplus reached NKr 105 billion (15 per cent of GDP), leading to a further increase in the current account surplus to NKr 27 billion (more than 4 per cent of GDP).

The large external surpluses since 1990 have been reflected in a sizeable decline in Norway's net foreign debt, from a level of over 20 per cent of GDP in 1988 to less than 10 per cent in 1992 (Diagram 8). Despite such a fall in external indebtedness and the reduction in interest rates, the balance of foreign investment income, which includes net interest payments, deteriorated further in 1992 (Diagram 8). This was mainly the result of a tax and accounting-reform-induced

Diagram 7. **THE CURRENT BALANCE AND ITS MAJOR COMPONENTS**
Billion kroner

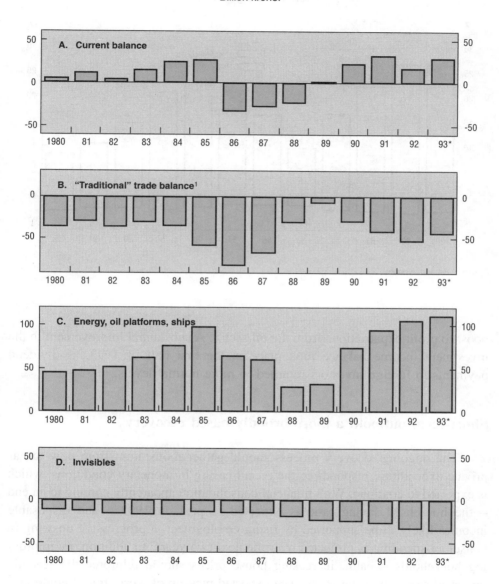

* First 6 months, seasonally adjusted, on an annual level.
1. Excluding exports and imports of petroleum, oil rigs and ships.
Source: Norwegian Central Bureau of Statistics.

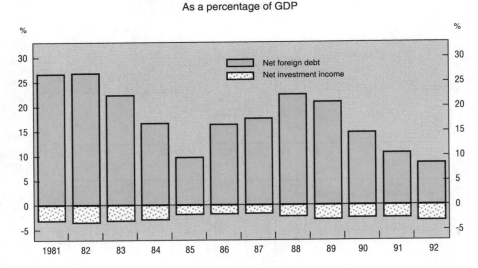

Source: Bank of Norway.

boost to profit expatriations from the oil sector. A substantial improvement in the investment income balance took place in the first half of 1993, as dividend payments to foreign investors returned to more normal levels.

Short-term outlook: a more broadly based recovery

The ongoing recovery process should gather momentum from now on, as private expenditure responds to the recent easing in monetary conditions, which is expected to continue. With financial consolidation apparently coming to an end – the household saving ratio is expected to peak in 1993 – and disposable incomes likely to be supported by rising employment, a progressive upswing in consumer spending is projected over the next two years. In addition, by improving households' wealth, increasing house prices should reinforce the recently observed rise in housing starts. The expected pick-up of world trade should also provide additional impetus to the Mainland economy by both ending the stagnation of non-energy exports and leading to an improvement in the terms of trade, thus generating income in the private sector. Given the rise in domestic and external demand, Mainland business investment is projected to recover progressively during 1994 and 1995. On the other hand, reductions in offshore investments are expected during that period, following the boom in recent years. All in all, Mainland growth is expected to accelerate from 1¾ percent in 1993 to 2¼ percent in 1994 and 3 per cent by 1995. As energy production is likely to expand strongly, somewhat higher growth rates are projected for total GDP (Table 5).

Despite such an expected improvement in growth performance, unemployment will probably decline only marginally: indeed increased employment oppor-

Table 5. **Short-term prospects** [1]

Percentage change, constant prices

	NKr billion in 1992	1993	1994	1995
Private consumption	365.0	1.7	2.5	3.0
Government consumption	157.4	3.0	2.2	2.0
Gross fixed investment [2]	137.7	3.4	0.3	5.0
of which:				
Oil sector [2]	45.1	15.0	−7.0	−5.0
Non-oil business sector	54.2	1.0	4.0	9.0
Residential construction	11.8	−4.0	7.0	10.0
Public sector	24.9	−10.0	0.0	2.0
Stockbuilding [3]	−9.7	0.0	0.0	0.0
Total domestic demand	650.4	2.3	2.0	3.1
Exports of goods and services	303.0	2.0	6.1	6.0
of which:				
Energy exports		6.0	9.0	5.0
Imports of goods and services	251.7	3.0	3.5	4.5
Foreign balance [4]	51.5	0.1	2.4	2.0
GDP	701.6	2.0	3.3	3.8
Memorandum items:				
Mainland GDP	584.3	1.8	2.3	3.0
Mainland GDP deflator		1.7	2.0	2.2
Private consumption deflator		2.3	1.8	2.1
Employment		0.0	0.7	1.3
Unemployment rate		6.0	5.9	5.7

1. Projections published in the *OECD Economic Outlook 54*, December 1993.
2. Includes platforms under construction.
3. Contribution to GDP growth, excluding platforms under construction.
4. Contribution to GDP growth.
Source: OECD.

tunities are likely to be reflected in some cyclical rebound of the labour force, while little further addition is expected as to the number of persons enrolled in active labour market programmes. At the same time, given the continued slack in product and labour markets, inflation should remain low, thus preserving recent gains in the cost competitiveness of export-oriented industries. As a result, with oil exports expected to grow rapidly and the terms of trade to improve somewhat, the current account surplus is projected to widen markedly, implying virtually an elimination of net foreign debt by 1995.

This set of projections is based on the following assumptions:

– The projected pick-up in OECD growth is expected to lead to Norwegian export market growth of 4½ and 6 per cent, respectively, in 1994 and 1995.

– The average OECD oil import price is expected to recover somewhat from US$15 per barrel in the second half of 1993 to US$15.8 in the second half of 1995.

– The projected easing in monetary conditions in Europe is expected to lead to further reductions of Norwegian short-term interest rates – to a level of 4 to 4.5 per cent by 1995 – while long-term rates will probably decline only marginally from their present level.

– Growth rates for energy exports are expected to remain roughly at the high level recorded recently, on average 6 to 7 per cent per annum.

– Real Government expenditure is expected to grow slightly less than Mainland GDP in 1994 and 1995. This implies a broadly constant structural non-oil deficit.

The main uncertainty attached to these projections lies with the expected world recovery, as Norwegian manufacturing export volumes and revenues are highly sensitive to cyclical and commodity price developments. Another uncertainty relates to the strength of consumer demand: by encouraging precautionary savings, the continuing weak employment situation could induce households to delay spending and hence adversely affect business confidence.

II. Economic policies

Overview

Since the floating of the Norwegian krone in late 1992, monetary conditions have eased considerably. While the exchange rate has stabilised after a limited initial depreciation, interest rates have declined steeply to below the levels recorded elsewhere in Europe. At the same time, fiscal policy has remained expansionary and the general Government deficit in 1993 is estimated to reach almost 3 per cent of GDP. The 1994 Budget calls for only a modest fiscal tightening, implying a persistently large non-oil deficit. Following major reforms in the fields of taxation and energy markets, most recent structural policy initiatives have essentially focused on domains related to the implementation of the European Economic Area (EEA) treaty, which was ratified by Norway in October 1992. An assessment of recent and prospective macroeconomic as well as structural policy developments (including an update on banking reform, which was examined in detail in the last year's Survey) is presented below.

Monetary management

Small exchange-rate depreciation since the krone's floating

Following the turmoil in European exchange markets, the Norwegian krone came under strong downward pressure during the Autumn of 1992. Despite heavy official interventions and steep increases in short-term interest rates to keep the fixed parity with the ecu, in the three weeks following the decision of the Swedish Government to let its currency float, the speculation intensified so that the Norwegian authorities suspended the krone-ecu link from 10 December 1992. In the immediate aftermath of these events the krone weakened somewhat, but it has remained stable since. This is in sharp contrast to developments in Finland and Sweden, which have seen their currencies depreciate sharply since floating (Diagram 9, panel A), due to the severe imbalances prevailing in these two countries.

Against the Deutschemark, the Norwegian krone has fallen by about 6 per cent over the past year or so, with most of the devaluation occurring in late 1992. In trade-weighted terms and against the ecu, the depreciation has been considerably smaller (Diagram 9, panel B) – about 3 to 4 per cent from November 1992 to December 1993 – as the currencies of a number of Norway's most important trading partners have also weakened against the Deutschemark. In fact, the krone would have been even stronger had the monetary authorities not used the considerable foreign currency inflow from late January as an opportunity to replenish foreign exchange reserves (Diagram 9, panel C). In the first half of 1993, the Bank of Norway bought foreign currency for the equivalent of NKr 57 billion ($8 billion), somewhat more than the amount it had sold to support the krone in late 1992. Since then, the central bank has intervened both ways, to maintain stability in the foreign exchange market. The unrest in European currency markets during the summer of 1993 left the Norwegian krone largely unaffected.

As regards the general orientation of exchange rate policy, the Government stated in December 1992 – just after the decision to float – its intention to reintroduce a fixed exchange rate regime as soon as international conditions permitted it. The central bank lent support to such a policy in an official statement in May 1993, but underlined that the present floating regime might continue for a considerable period of time and that a fixed exchange rate regime would be workable only within the context of "close and binding international co-operation". Although the credibility of monetary policy has not suffered from the decision to let the krone float, the issue has been raised by the Bank of Norway as to whether – following the example of Sweden, Finland and other countries which have recently floated their currency – the adoption of an alternative nominal anchor for monetary policy, such as inflation targets, would be appropriate. This issue is currently being investigated. At the same time, the need to keep price and wage increases below those of trading partners has been underlined, which has been reflected in a close shadowing of the ecu in managing the krone's exchange rate.

Diagram 9. **EXCHANGE RATE BEHAVIOUR AND OFFICIAL RESERVES**

January 1992 = 100

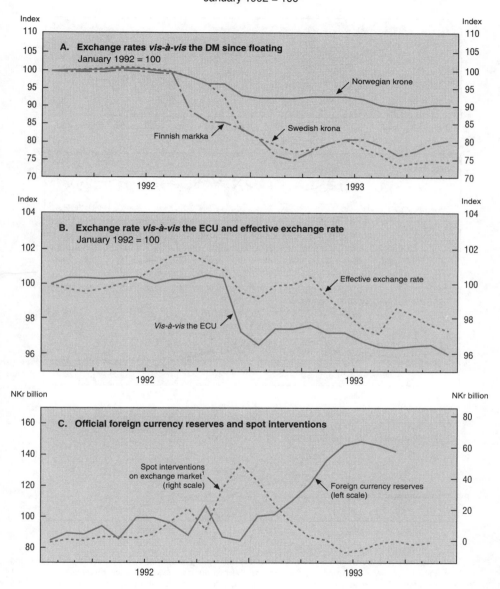

1. Net accumulated sales of currency to banks from January 1992 onwards.
Sources: Bank of Norway; Norwegian Central Bureau of Statistics.

Diagram 10. **INTEREST RATE DEVELOPMENTS**

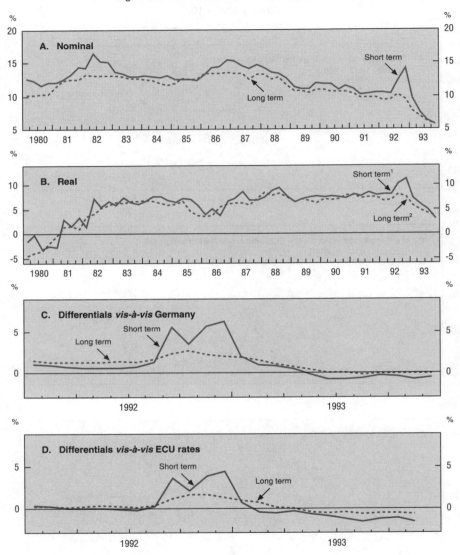

1. 3-month Nibor rate less the expected rate of inflation, the latter being measured by the percentage change in the CPI (at annual rate) over the quarter preceding and the two quarters following each observation.
2. Yield of long-term Government bonds less the expected rate of inflation, the latter being measured by the percentage change in the CPI over the 4 quarters following each observation.
    For 1994, OECD projections for the CPI are used.
Sources: IMF, *International Financial Statistics;* OECD, *Main Economic Indicators.*

Marked easing in monetary conditions

The limited depreciation of the krone since its floating, combined with declining European interest rate levels, has permitted a substantial easing in domestic monetary conditions. With a view to retaining financial-market confidence and, as noted above, reconstituting international reserves, the Bank of Norway has followed a cautious policy of repeated small cuts in interest rates. Nonetheless, by mid-1993 the short-term "floor" rate[5] had been reduced to 5.5 per cent, as compared with a pre-floating level of 16 per cent. Following further cuts in European interest rates, central bank rates were reduced by another 50 basis points during the autumn. As a result, short-term interest rates – nominal and real – are now at historically low levels (Diagram 10, panels A and B). Long-term rates have also dropped significantly, with the yield for nine-year bonds below 6 per cent from October 1993, implying a broadly flat yield curve. Differentials *vis-à-vis* Deutschemark and ecu rates have fallen below the levels experienced prior to the currency crisis, turning negative in late spring (Diagram 10, panels C and D).

Improved bank profitability but still weak bank lending

The balance sheets of commercial and savings banks for the first three quarters 1993 show a further improvement in profitability, with commercial banks recording positive operating results (after loan losses) for the first time since 1989 (Table 6).[6] The markedly better economic environment along with easing monetary conditions has led to a significant reduction of loan losses since 1991. This trend is likely to have been sustained during 1993: the fall in bankruptcies, and hence potential bank losses, already observed in the first three quarters of this year is an indicator of this (Diagram 11, panels A and B). Moreover, the reduction in bank branches and staff since 1990 has been reflected in lower operating costs (Diagram 11, panel C).

Capital gains on bond holdings, due to falling interest rates, have also temporarily boosted banks' operating results (Table 6). By contrast, banks have not increased their margins, which have remained relatively stable during 1993 and have fallen somewhat since 1989. While some fluctuations have occurred in the differential between their short-term loan rates and marginal funding costs (the latter measured by three-month money market rates), the gap between loan rates and sight deposits has remained within a band of 5 to

Table 6. **Banks' balance sheets**

Per cent of average total assets

A. **Commercial banks**[1]

	1989	1990	1991	1992	1993 1st three quarters
Net interest revenues	3.0	2.6	2.5	2.8	3.0
Other operating revenues	1.4	1.1	0.9	1.1	1.5
Operating costs	2.7	2.9	3.3	2.9	2.5
Operating profits before losses	1.6	0.8	0.0	1.0	2.0
Loan losses[2]	1.6	2.0	4.3	2.3	1.5
Operating profits after losses	0.0	-1.2	-4.3	-1.3	0.5
Memorandum item:					
Capital adequacy ratio[3]	8.6	8.5	7.1	8.6	

B. **Savings banks**[4]

	1989	1990	1991	1992	1993 1st three quarters
Net interest revenues	4.1	3.9	3.8	4.3	4.6
Other operating revenues	1.1	0.7	0.6	0.8	1.5
Operating costs	3.3	3.3	3.5	3.3	3.0
Operating profits before losses	1.9	1.3	0.9	1.9	3.1
Loan losses	2.2	2.1	2.1	1.8	1.2
Operating profits after losses	-0.3	-0.8	-1.2	0.1	1.9
Memorandum item:					
Capital adequacy ratio[3]	5.9	6.1	7.8	10.5	

1. Not consolidated with non-bank subsidiaries.
2. Includes losses resulting from bank guarantees.
3. BIS standards from 1991 onwards.
4. 24 largest savings banks.
Source: Bank of Norway.

7 percentage points (Diagram 12, panels A and B). The banks have, however, sought to improve their net interest income by shifting the funding of loans towards deposits and away from more costly money market resources. At the same time, the fall in interest rates has reduced the financing costs of non-performing loans.

The broad stability of lending spreads along with the continued sluggishness of fixed capital formation suggests that the banks' credit behaviour over the past year or so (Diagram 12, panel C) has been dominated by demand weakness rather

Diagram 11. **BANKING SITUATION**

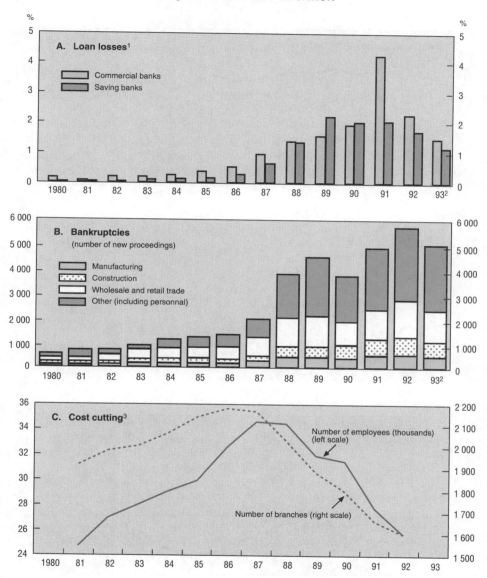

1. As a percentage of average assets.
2. First three quarters of 1993.
3. Commercial and saving banks.
Source: Bank of Norway.

Diagram 12. **BANK LENDING**

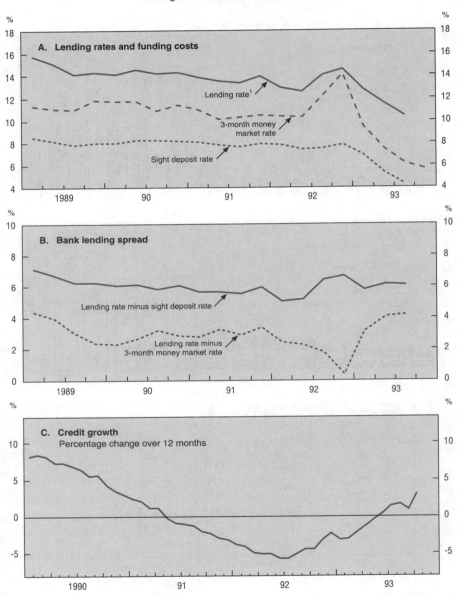

A. **Lending rates and funding costs**

Lending rate[1]

3-month money market rate

Sight deposit rate

B. **Bank lending spread**

Lending rate minus sight deposit rate

Lending rate minus 3-month money market rate

C. **Credit growth**
Percentage change over 12 months

1. Rate on short-term loans by commercial banks.
Sources: Bank of Norway; OECD, *Main Economic Indicators.*

36

Table 7. **Sources of domestic credit expansion**

Percentage change from previous year

	Level end 1991 NKr bill.	1990	1991	1992	1993[1]
Commercial and savings banks[2]	386.3	3.2	−2.2	−1.6[4]	3.7
State banks[3]	171.7	6.7	8.2	6.5	0.1
Private finance companies	19.6	−16.2	−3.2	−11.4	−0.3
Non-life insurance companies	4.3	−19.8	3.7	41.9	13.2
Life insurance companies, pension funds	74.2	4.4	13.5	10.6	−3.6
Mortgage institutions	104.1	−0.6	−19.1	−20.9[4]	−16.5
Bond and certificate market[5]	64.0	20.1	6.1	−0.6	15.9
Inter-company loans	11.4	−19.3	−30.1	−34.2	−33.0
Other credit	0.6	−22.2	−2.6	3.8	−1.5
Total domestic credit	836.2	3.1	−1.6	−1.2	0.8

1. October 1992 to October 1993 at annual rates.
2. Including the Postal Savings Banks.
3. Excluding loans of Municipal Bank.
4. Growth rates for 1992 are adjusted for the conversion of Bolig og Naringskreditt A/s from a mortgage institution to a bank in autumn 1992.
5. Adjusted for non-residents' holdings of private and municipal bonds issued in Norway.
Source: Bank of Norway.

than by supply constraints. While credit extension by commercial and savings banks has shown a modest recovery recently – growing by 3-4 per cent in the 12 months to October 1993 – lending by other financial institutions is in general still declining (Table 7). The major exception has been the state banks, which – through their subsidised loan rates – have been able to expand market shares considerably (*e.g.* they have increased their share of mortgage lending from 70 to 90 per cent in recent years).

Rapid growth of monetary aggregates

The credit squeeze in recent years has happened alongside a relatively rapid expansion of monetary aggregates, well in excess of nominal income growth in the Mainland economy (Table 8). The increasing public deficits – financed mainly through a reduction of the state's deposits at the central bank – have been the major source of money growth.[7] This has been partly offset by less credit granted by the domestic private-sector financial system (as noted above, state banks have continued to expand lending). More recently, the sources of monetary

37

Table 8. **Money growth**

Per cent

	1990	1991	1992	1993[1]
M1 (change from previous year)[2]	10.5	6.8	8.6	12.3
M2 (change from previous year)[3]	6.0	10.6	7.3	4.9
Contribution from:				
Banks' net foreign assets[4]	–0.9	–3.3	–0.6	2.8
Domestic sources	6.9	13.9	7.9	2.0
of which:				
Credit to central government[5]	8.8	10.3	11.4	3.2
State bank credit to the private sector[6]	1.9	2.6	2.0	0.6
Other bank credit to the private sector	0.2	2.7	–5.3	–0.6
Miscellaneous[7]	–4.0	–1.9	0.1	–1.2

1. From 30 September 1992 to 30 September 1993.
2. Currency, demand deposits and unused credit held by the public.
3. M1 plus time deposits.
4. Includes lending to the public denominated in foreign currency and the public net sale of foreign currency to banks (exclusive of sales related to payment of oil taxes).
5. Includes reduced government deposits at the central bank, but excludes net new issues of government bonds and oil taxes.
6. Excluding credit supplied by nationalised commercial and savings banks.
7. Unspecified items and statistical discrepancy.
Source: Bank of Norway.

expansion have changed somewhat: the inflow of foreign currency following the floating of the krone, together with the recent revival of bank lending, has boosted money growth; by contrast, the contribution from the central Government (including loan transactions) has fallen.

The fiscal stance

Continued budget stimulus in 1992-93

The expansionary fiscal stance initiated in 1989 was pursued in 1992 and 1993, leading to a cumulated stimulus of nearly 8 per cent of Mainland GDP over the past five years as measured by the change in the cyclically-adjusted budget balance net of oil revenues and interest payments (Diagram 13, panel B). The worsening in the Government's fiscal position is mainly attributable to rapidly increasing outlays. As can be seen from Table 9, in recent years total public expenditures have grown well in excess of, and revenues somewhat less than,

Diagram 13. **STATE BUDGET BALANCE**
As a percentage of Mainland GDP

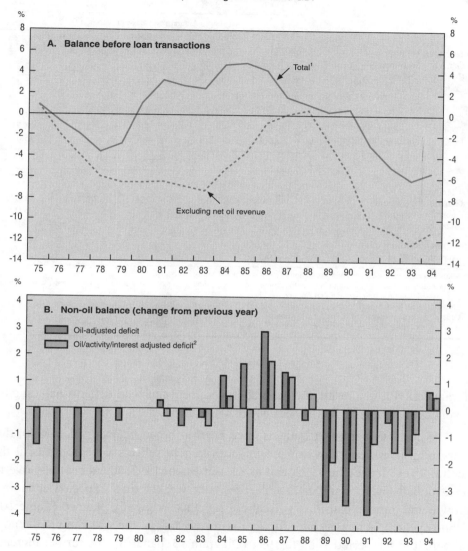

Note: Data for 1992 and 1993 are estimates; for 1994, projections.
1. As a percentage of total GDP.
2. Adjusted for cyclical developments, petroleum income, foreign interest payments, capital transactions and transfers from the Bank of Norway.
Source: Norwegian Ministry of Finance.

Table 9. **Government expenditure, revenue and net lending position**

	1990	1991	1992	1993[1]	1994[1]
	Annual percentage growth				
Total expenditure:[2]					
General government	6.2	7.4	6.4	5.8	2.8
Central government	7.9	7.4	7.0	6.5	2.6
Local government	2.2	5.0	3.5	1.1	3.4
Total revenue:[2]					
General government	8.9	2.0	1.4	3.9	2.7
Central government	9.6	3.4	−0.8	2.7	3.7
Local government	6.9	5.3	4.3	1.9	3.0
	Level, percentage of GDP				
Net lending:[3]					
General government	2.6	−0.2	−2.8	−2.7	−3.0
Central government	2.8	0.0	−2.7	−2.8	−3.0
Local government	−0.2	−0.2	0.0	0.1	0.0
Memorandum item:					
Nominal GDP growth	6.3	4.0	2.2	4.1[4]	3.6[4]

1. Ministry of Finance estimates and projections (1994 budget, December version).
2. Figures are calculated according to National Accounts definitions, though, for central and local governments, with revenues and expenditure on administrative and not accrual basis.
3. Figures are on SNA basis.
4. Official projection contained in the 1994 National Budget (December version).
Source: Norwegian Ministry of Finance, the 1994 National Budget (October and December versions).

nominal GDP. As a result, the general Government financial deficit (including oil revenues) has approached 3 per cent of GDP.

As local Government budgets have been in broad balance since 1990, this worsening in general Government finances largely reflects developments at the central level.[8] Indeed, in 1992, and to a lesser extent 1993, actual central Government deficits were significant, reflecting both weaker than expected economic growth and more expansionary fiscal policies than originally planned (Table 10). While cyclical factors account for approximately half of the widening in the non-oil deficit in the period 1989 to 1991 (Diagram 13, panel B), the further increase since can be entirely attributed to discretionary actions, as reflected in the deterioration in the structural budget balance by about 2½ percent of Mainland GDP (Table 10). The most important discretionary measures have been the strengthening of active labour market programmes (see Part III) and the 1992 tax reform

Table 10. **State budget balance: projections and outcomes**

	1992		1993		1994
	Budget	Outcome	Budget	Estimated outcome[5]	Budget
	Percentage of total GDP				
Budget balance before loan transactions	−3.5	−5.0	−6.8	−6.3	−6.1
	Percentage of mainland GDP				
Oil-adjusted budget balance[1]	−9.9	−11.2	−12.5	−12.4	−11.7
Revenues[2]	45.6	47.1	45.7	45.8	45.8
Expenditures[3]	55.5	58.3	58.2	58.3	57.5
Change in structural budget balance[4]	−1.3	−1.6	−0.3	−0.9	0.5
Memorandum items:					
Local government balance, percent of GDP	0.0	0.0	−0.1	0.1	0.0
Mainland GDP growth underlying budget estimates and outcomes, percent changes	2.6	2.0	1.8	1.3	1.7

1. Before loan transactions, adjusted for government net oil revenues.
2. Excluding oil revenues.
3. Excluding expenditures related to central government oil activities.
4. Adjusted for cyclical developments, petroleum income, foreign interest payments, capital transactions and transfers from the Bank of Norway.
5. Ministry of Finance estimation, December 1993.
Source: Norwegian Ministry of Finance, *National Budgets.*

(leading to an estimated net revenue loss of NKr 5.6 billion or 0.9 per cent of Mainland GDP). As a result, the State budget deficit, net of oil-related revenues and expenditures, which had reached 10½ percent of Mainland GDP in 1991, has continued to rise, approaching 12½ per cent in 1993. Including oil-related budget items, the deficit has shown a similar upward trend but at a lower level (Diagram 13, panel A).

Fiscal tightening envisaged for 1994

The need for fiscal retrenchment after several years of continued deterioration of public finances is reflected in the draft State budget for 1994. The proposed increase in non-oil expenditure – 2 per cent in nominal terms – is well below the trend of recent years and the expected growth in nominal Mainland GDP. In line with the Government's stated policy to shift expenditure from transfers to infrastructure investments broadly defined, reductions of direct subsidies to households (corresponding to ½ percent of Mainland GDP) are envisaged. In particular, reimbursement of medical bills will be reduced, and tighter control of eligibility for sickness pay and unemployment benefits is to be introduced. Altogether, this is estimated to reduce the real growth of transfers to households by 1 percentage point. In addition, support to primary industries is to be curtailed. Other discretionary increases in spending include measures to further upgrade active labour market polices and strengthen industrial competitiveness (through support to small- and medium-sized enterprises).

State revenues will be boosted by a sizeable increase in profit payments by the central bank (corresponding to $3/4$ percent of Mainland GDP) and other public entities. Non-oil taxes are expected to increase by $3^1/2$ percent, in line with the projected nominal expansion of the Mainland economy, following several years of somewhat slower growth. Tax thresholds will, in general, be raised in line with the official projection of a 2 per cent increase in wage rates. The two major discretionary changes in the tax system proposed in the 1994 budget – the abolition of electricity taxes for industry and an increase in the wealth tax – would reduce and boost respectively tax receipts by 0.5 and 1.3 per cent of Mainland GDP.

The State budget deficit, excluding oil-related items, is projected to decrease from an estimated 12.4 per cent of Mainland GDP (NKr 74.7 billion) in 1993 to 11.7 per cent (NKr 72.5 billion) in 1994, implying a slight reduction in the oil, activity and interest-adjusted deficit (Table 10 and Diagram 9, panel B). The projected improvement in the total State budget position (including oil) is of the same order of magnitude, as the net revenue contribution from petroleum activities remains roughly constant (falling oil receipts, partly a result of lower oil prices, are offset by a decline in state oil investments). On a national accounts basis, though, the 1994 budget implies practically unchanged central and general Government deficits (Table 9).[9]

Risks of unsustainability in the long term

In February 1993, the Government presented a new "Long-Term Programme" for the period 1994-97, reflecting the concern that the rapid deterioration in public finances in recent years is becoming unsustainable. Accordingly, the Programme recognised that employment creation could no longer be pursued through expansionary fiscal policies.

Previous "Long-Term Programmes" had already drawn attention to the need for restraining public spending and in particular transfers, whose growth has outstripped by far that of total public expenditure. Since the Autumn of 1990, some measures to this end have been implemented, implying a reduction of transfers by about 1 per cent of Mainland GDP. Nonetheless, public transfers (even excluding unemployment compensation) have continued to expand much faster than other expenditure items (Diagram 14, panel A) and economic growth, exceeding previous projections by a wide margin.[10] Over the last three decades, Government expenditure growth has consistently been above projections, with public consumption expanding on average 1 to 2 per cent per year more than planned (Diagram 14, panel B).[11]

As part of a "solidarity alternative" programme (see Part III) the "Employment Commission"[12] recommended to reduce the underlying trend growth in transfers by an amount equivalent to $3/4$ percent of Mainland GDP (NKr 5 billion). Along these lines, the draft Budget for 1994 contains discretionary gross cuts in transfers to households of NKr 3 billion (with the rest planned for 1995). However, even a full implementation of the Employment Commission proposals would not suffice to tackle the long-term challenges facing Norwegian public finances. With demographic developments tending to boost transfer payments over the coming decades, and a non-oil budget deficit in excess of the Government's own estimates of both medium-term and permanent oil income,[13] a significant tightening of fiscal policy is clearly warranted. At present, such a need is far from being fulfilled. Indeed, the most recent official projections of public finances consistent with the policy assumptions retained by the Commission imply a more or less unchanged non-oil central Government deficit (amounting to more than 11 per cent of Mainland GDP) over the period 1994-97, contrasting with the permanent oil income to Government of roughly 7 per cent of Mainland GDP (Diagram 15, panel A).

It is, of course, difficult to predict with any confidence the future Government revenues from oil: a mere 15 per cent deviation of the crude oil price from the base line assumption leads to a change in oil income by roughly 30 per cent (Diagram 15, panel A). Given the volatility of the oil price (in January 1994, it was down to NKr 107 or $14 per barrel), such deviations in either direction are certainly not excluded. It would, however, appear imprudent to base future fiscal policies upon the hope that a strong rebound in oil prices might close the present deficit.

Diagram 14. **PUBLIC EXPENDITURE**

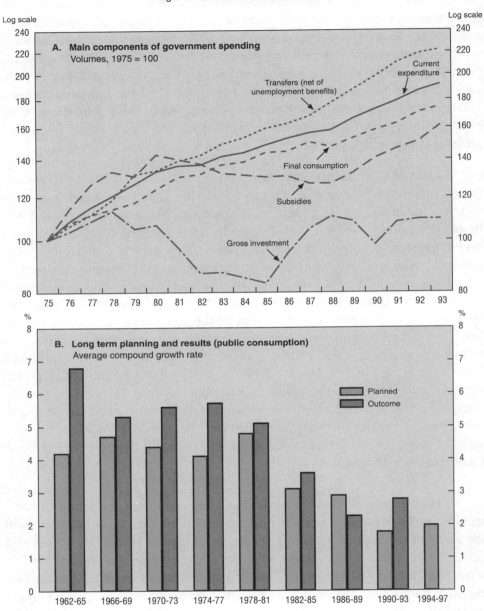

Sources: Norwegian Ministry of Finance and OECD.

44

Diagram 15. **FISCAL SUSTAINABILITY**

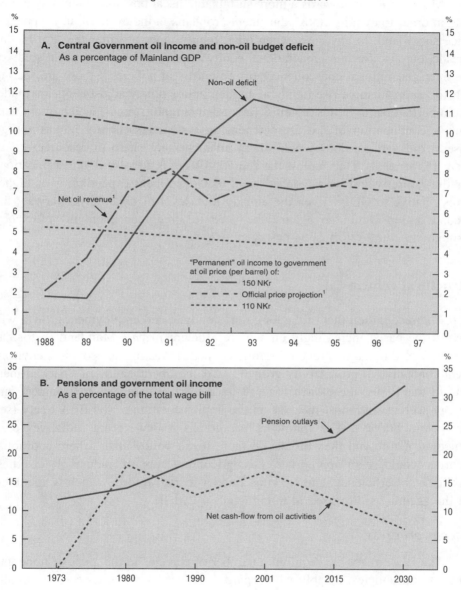

1. Assuming, in 1994 prices, an oil price of 120 NKr per barrel from 1994 to 1997, followed by 134 from 1998 onwards.
Sources: Government Long-term Programme, 1994-1997; submissions from Ministry of Finance; OECD.

45

Moving rapidly towards a more sustainable fiscal position is not only advisable in order to avoid serious adjustment problems in the event of an adverse oil price shock and, in any case, when oil revenues taper off after the turn of this decade, but also for inter-generational equity considerations. In a recent study of the inter-generational consequences of present fiscal policies,[14] these are seen to call for a considerable rise in the tax burden unless policy adjustments are made. An important factor in this regard is future demographic trends, which imply that, with a continuation of the present pension system (essentially pay-as-you-go based), old age pensions would claim an increasing share of resources (Diagram 15, panel B). Thus, unless the deficit problem is addressed, the implications for the future would be a reduced level of Government expenditures or higher taxes relative to GDP. Given the already high level of taxation in Norway, the second option would go against the need to strengthen economic efficiency through structural reforms, as described below.

Structural reform

The recognition that in the long run economic and employment growth will have to be based increasingly on a more efficient *private* Mainland sector has been reflected in major structural reforms aimed at creating an economic environment conducive to productivity growth. After the liberalisation of financial markets in the 1980s, these have focused on the tax system, the environment and energy sectors, and most recently on the implementation of the EEA treaty (see last year's Survey). The following paragraphs review recent initiatives of a structural nature and then discuss in more detail policy areas where additional reforms would seem appropriate, *i.e.* agricultural support, industrial subsidies, public-sector efficiency, and banking. Labour-market reform, which is also high on the agenda, is discussed in more detail in Part III.

Recent progress

The EEA treaty has required a number of changes in the areas of trade and competition policies, notably with regard to industrial support, access to public procurement and restrictions on foreign ownership of enterprises and real estate. In addition, a body of legislation, effective from January 1994, *inter alia*, reduces current price controls and limits price collusion, bringing competition regulation into greater conformity with EC principles. In the area of air transport, both the July 1992 agreement between Norway, Sweden and the EC and the implementation of the EEA treaty should greatly increase competitive pressures; some restrictions concerning cabotage – *i.e.* foreign companies' right to compete with purely domestic flights – will remain in place until April 1997, however.

In order to improve the supply of capital to small and medium-sized enterprises, three large state investment funds have been merged, effective from 1 January 1993. The main function of the new entity will be the provision of long-term capital, either in the form of equity or loans, often at subsidised rates. More generally, increased emphasis is to be put on improving incentives for research and development. Though the new fund is under the administration of a national authority,[15] the disbursement of capital is to a large extent delegated to local development centres with considerable autonomy and an explicit regional development dimension. It is too early to tell whether such recent initiatives have enhanced the efficiency of Government support to businesses.

In a bill adopted by Parliament in February 1993, the Government proposed a revision of the principles and framework for Norwegian agricultural policies. At this stage, it is difficult to predict to what extent the stated objectives – to increase efficiency while promoting more environmentally sound practices – will in practice lead to increased market orientation. (The system and level of agricultural support are discussed below.) As regards fisheries, the amount of subsidies has been reduced considerably since 1990, and in the latest "Long-Term Programme", referred to above, an almost complete phasing out of support to this sector will be achieved by 1997.

There have been a number of initiatives aimed at reducing the costs firms face in complying with public regulation. Two Government committees are currently reviewing the existing stock of legislation in order to identify superfluous or unnecessarily complicated regulations. While the work is as yet in its initial stages, some concrete proposals have been put forward, such as simplifying the process of obtaining building permits and reducing the number of public entities to which firms have to provide information of a legal or statistical character.

To facilitate efficient decision making, larger autonomy has been granted to public institutions, in particular those that produce services sold to the public.[16] Entities mainly servicing the public sector itself have also been subject to less direct management control from central authorities. As recognised in the latest "Long-Term Programme" and State Budget, for such reforms to have a beneficial effect on efficiency, the existing direct control procedures would need to be replaced by other measures which evaluate the performance in terms of productivity and value of the services provided on an ongoing basis.

While the reduction in non-wage labour costs (see Part I) has improved the competitiveness of Norwegian firms, other recent initiatives in the area of taxation could partly reverse the positive effects of earlier tax reforms. In particular, although applicable to less than 1 per cent of the working population, the decision to raise marginal tax rates for high wage earners will lift the top rate on wage income from 55.8 to 59.4 per cent.[17] Moreover, the increase in the wealth tax, proposed in the State Budget for 1994, presents some problematic aspects. While the threshold for the imposition of this tax is low, the tax base is rather narrow. The tax favours institutional savings,[18] shareholdings and real investments (housing etc.), as opposed to bank deposits and bonds held directly by households. As it stands, with an increase in the marginal tax rate from 1.3 to 1.8 per cent of net wealth, such a measure would effectively raise the marginal capital income tax rate on bank deposits and bonds from 51.6 to about 60.7 per cent,[19] even for persons with rather modest financial wealth. While increasing the burden on some tax payers who are in a net wealth position, this could aggravate the existing problems with the distorted tax base and lead to increased tax arbitrage.

Possible additional reforms

Agricultural support

As measured by the Producer Subsidy Equivalent (PSE), the Norwegian agricultural sector is one of the most subsidised in the OECD area, benefiting from a support roughly three-quarters above the OECD average (Table 11). Indeed, the direct support from the State budget to agriculture – NKr 12.2 billion in 1993 – equals about NKr 150 000 per full-time worker. In addition, import restrictions tend to raise domestic food prices, as evidenced in the high level of the implicit tax on consumer purchases (CSE). Given the fact that less-well-off families tend to spend a larger proportion of their disposable income on food, such a system of agricultural support also tends to be regressive in its effect on income distribution.

Table 11. **Agricultural support in Norway**

	1990	1991	1992
Assistance to producers (PSE)			
Total NKr billion	18.9	19.8	18.9
Total US$ billion	3.0	3.1	3.1
Percentage PSE	74	77	77
Ratio to OECD, percentage PSE	1.72	1.75	1.75
Implicit tax on consumers (CSE)			
Total NKr billion	9.9	9.9	9.7
Total US$ billion	1.59	1.53	1.57
Percentage CSE	65	65	63
Ratio to OECD, percentage CSE	1.80	1.75	1.75

Source: *Agricultural Policies, Markets and Trade. Monitoring and Outlook*, OECD, 1993.

In a report on potential efficiency gains resulting from reforms of the public sector,[20] it was estimated that Norwegian agricultural production could be maintained at present levels with about 20 000 employed – one-fifth of the actual workforce – if it was reallocated to the most efficient farms. In addition, simplified support schemes resulting from such a reform would lead to savings in compliance costs corresponding to 12 000 full-time employed in the public and private sector. While such calculations can only be indicative, they certainly demonstrate that non-economic objectives – in particular preserving agricultural activity in areas with difficult production conditions – are achieved at very high costs to the economy.

The challenge in reforming the system thus lies in the attainment of well-defined non-economic objectives at increased levels of efficiency in the use of resources. In this perspective, a recent study[21] considers different scenarios, which explicitly take into account the need to respect certain social constraints when meeting alternative agricultural policy objectives, namely self-sufficiency in a food crisis, compatibility with the GATT-round proposals of the time and possible EC membership. In the simulation of self-sufficiency, present population levels in distant regions are not allowed to decline by more than 50 per cent. The results summarised in Table 12 show that even total self-sufficiency in a food crisis could be obtained with significantly lower use of resources. While the successful conclusion of the GATT-round should be less drastic in consequences, the simulations indicate that a ''pure'' implementation of even the present EC

Table 12. **Effects of agricultural reforms**

Change from base year (1990)

	Self-sufficiency "reform"[1]	GATT round implemented	EC membership without modification[2]
Per cent reduction in:			
Employment	54	22	65
Land use	46	30	43
Reduction of total support (NKr billion)	12.1	6.5	14.1
of which:			
Market price support	7.5	2.3	5.5
Budget support	4.6	4.2	8.6

1. Defined as a reform where agriculture support is reduced to the level necessary to maintain an agricultural sector that could provide adequate food supply in a crisis situation, when imports are cut off.
2. The calculations of the consequences of EC membership are shown as mid-range estimates. "Without modification" means that no concessions are made to Norway in the case of actual EC membership.
Source: "Agriculture as a provider of public goods", Rolf Brunstad *et al.*, 1993.

agricultural system and support levels would necessitate a considerable downsizing of agriculture in Norway.

In its position paper on Norway's application for membership,[22] the Commission of the European Community acknowledged that underlying objectives in Norwegian agricultural policies – primarily to prevent depopulation of rural areas – are to a large extent compatible with current EC arrangements. The main problem arises from the fact that the Norwegian regions concerned are not "poor" enough to qualify for aid, and that difficult conditions in arctic areas have not yet been recognised as specific support criteria in EC policies.[23]

Industrial subsidies

Though agriculture accounts for about 50 per cent of Government subsidies, the level of support to manufacturing is not insignificant, exceeding (on SNA-definitions) 9 per cent of value added in that sector. This is to be compared with an EC average of 3.5 per cent. The bulk goes to shipbuilding, corresponding in 1993 to one-third of value added or roughly NKr 100 000 per employee. The indicators of industrial support signal a clear need for overhauling Norwegian policy in this area, with – as in the case of agriculture – an emphasis on achieving social objectives at considerable less cost to the economy. Such a need would be accentuated by EC-membership, as the European Commission in the paper referred to above specifically mentioned industrial subsidies as a potentially contentious issue.

Public sector efficiency

The steady increase in the public sector's share in total employment and GDP has drawn attention to the question of the efficiency with which resources are used. At the same time, the future public spending constraints discussed above have underlined the necessity to reassess priorities. For example, given the ageing population, it would seem sensible to cut resources in primary education to provide for increased expenditure on pensions, health care for the elderly, etc. So far, an ever rising number of teachers has provided education to a steadily declining population of children. Perhaps somewhat surprisingly, this has not resulted in increased services available per student (except for the integration of disabled in ordinary schools), but has been offset by reductions in working time and improved working conditions for teachers. Looking at data from individual schools, it appears that those schools which have experienced the largest reductions in pupil-to-teacher ratios are simply the ones with the largest decreases in the number of pupils.[24] In other words, the fall in the ratios has apparently not been the result of efforts to raise quality, but rather the consequence of an inability to reduce resource use when the number of pupils declines.

Another public area where there seems to be considerable scope for reform is the health sector. A study on unit costs in four major hospitals[25] found considerable differences in terms of average cost per patient, average number of patient days and costs per patient days. Spending per patient day, for instance, differs by one-third among the hospitals considered. While such comparisons of health costs are fraught with difficulties – in particular because of differences in quality – the study suggests that there is considerable room for cost reductions by adopting best practices: a reduction of costs to the lowest recorded level is broadly estimated to generate savings in the magnitude of NKr 450 million at 1990 prices.

In summary, there is ample evidence of potential efficiency gains in the provision of public services. More use could be made of market-oriented instruments – such as provision of vouchers to the final consumers for financing education needs, grants to public ''enterprises'' based on output measures etc.[26] Also, to keep up the momentum of regulatory reform aimed at reducing business compliance costs, it might be useful, as in some other OECD countries, to evaluate systematically new legislation – and where appropriate old legislation – in terms of its resulting cost and benefits for the private and public sector.

Banking reform

The improved profitability of commercial and savings banks observed recently (see above) now gives the Government the opportunity of moving from crisis management to reform of the banking sector.[27] The subsidy which had been provided to the banks through the Bank of Norway's low-rate deposit was discontinued at the end of November 1993. A next step would be to begin the privatisation of the major commercial banks, which, because of the huge Government support during the crisis, have become fully or partly State-owned.

As argued in last year's Survey, a continued dominant Government involvement in the banking industry would not be a desirable structure of Governance in the long run from the viewpoint of an efficient allocation of capital. Hence, the necessity of facilitating the return of private capital into banking. Evidently, such a process of bank privatisation must be assessed case-by-case as the nationalised financial institutions have not progressed at the same pace in terms of restructuring and adjustments in balance sheets. The current strategy of the authorities – consistent with the suggestions made in the previous Survey – is to proceed, in a first instance, with partial cessions of banks' capital through new share issues into the private sector,[28] so that benchmark values for further sales of bank shares can be established. In so doing, however, a clearer statement of the authorities' intentions, demonstrating their resolve to abandon major positions in the banking industry, might be helpful to increase confidence among potential investors.

In moving towards privatisation, however, a rationalisation of the whole banking sector would be required to create the grounds for a lean and efficient financial system. In this regard, it would seem appropriate to reassess the present role of the traditional state banks. While the primary function of these institutions has been to provide cheap finance to households for residential investments, student loans etc., their increasing activities have led to distortions in competition within the banking system. At the very least, state banks' operations should be limited to those that fulfil well defined social objectives. It must also be stressed that the expansion of the recently created "Post Bank" – which is well capitalised – is potentially an additional element giving state financial institutions a competitive edge over commercial and saving banks.

III. The labour market: performance and scope for reform

By traditional measures, Norway's labour market performance has been outstanding for much of the last thirty years. Within the confines of a small open economy, Norwegians developed a set of institutions and policies which, for many years, enabled the country to have one of the lowest unemployment rates in the OECD. However, since the mid-1980s the labour market situation has deteriorated (Diagram 16). Although, as compared to other OECD countries, Norway's current unemployment rate is still low (just over 6 per cent on a standardised basis), its unprecedented and persistent rise (nearly 300 per cent) is disconcerting. In fact, if workers on various Government programmes were taken into account, the extent of labour market slack would be significantly larger than suggested by the recorded unemployment rate. This raises the question whether those institutional and policy features which seemed to serve so well in the past are fully suited to today's economic environment.

To contain the growth in unemployment, Norwegian authorities have been pursuing an expansionary fiscal policy since the late 1980s, with Government deficits reaching unsustainable levels. Consequently, as recognised in the State Budget for 1994, any further fiscal boost to reduce unemployment appears inappropriate, the more so since, as stressed in previous Surveys, the rapid deterioration in Norwegian labour market conditions is not purely cyclical. Indeed, although the collapse of demand in 1987 played an important role, symptoms of rising unemployment were visible well before. In particular, a number of labour market institutions and Government programmes developed and refined during the 1960s and 1970s, when the Norwegian economy was more regulated and less integrated internationally, may have affected the country's ability to adapt to external shocks. Hence the need for reforms to improve the functioning of the labour market.

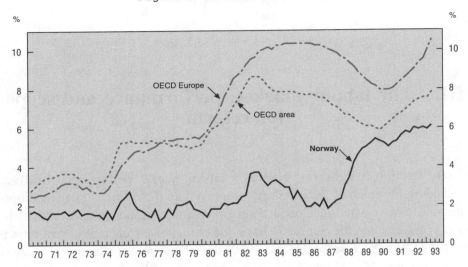

Diagram 16. **UNEMPLOYMENT RATES**

OECD Europe

OECD area

Norway

Source: OECD, *Main Economic Indicators.*

The present chapter focuses on recent labour market performance and the influence of Government policy on employment outcomes. Major symptoms of rising structural unemployment are first analysed. The extent to which Norway's wage bargaining system has been able to deliver sufficient real wage flexibility to cope with rising unemployment is then examined. This is followed by a discussion of how a number of labour market programmes may have affected the adjustment process through their impact on labour supply and by reducing the opportunity cost of unemployment. Prospects for reform are subsequently addressed.

Symptoms of rising structural unemployment

Unemployment in Norway remained very low for most of the last two decades, rarely rising above 2 per cent and showing no discernible upward trend prior to the mid-1980s (see Diagram 16). Until then, employment growth was strong while labour force participation grew from about 70 per cent to just under 80 per cent, largely fuelled by increasing participation by women (Diagram 17,

54

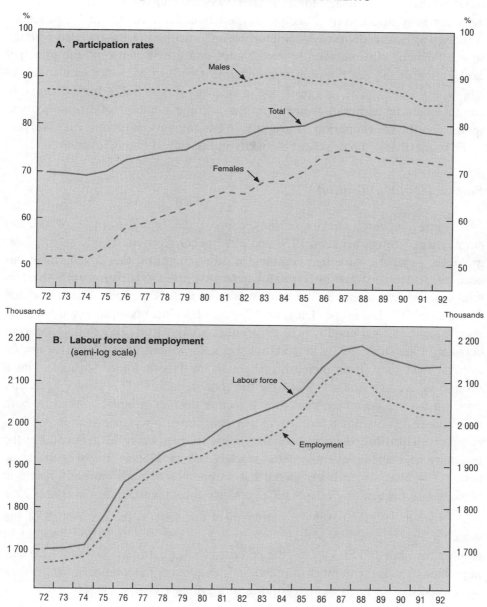

Diagram 17. **LABOUR SUPPLY DEVELOPMENTS**

A. **Participation rates**

Males

Total

Females

B. **Labour force and employment**
(semi-log scale)

Labour force

Employment

Source: OECD.

55

panel A). The rise in unemployment after 1986 coincided with a fall in employment not fully matched by a decline in the labour force (Diagram 17, panel B). Although aggregate demand developments (in particular those associated with the severe financial consolidation by households and firms) constitute the principal explanation of the deterioration in employment performance, the secular fall in labour utilisation rates suggests the existence of structural impediments to employment. In addition, increase in the average duration of unemployment spells, and the concentration of unemployment among low productivity workers – are suggestive of non-cyclical elements in the rise in unemployment.

Fall in labour utilisation

Aggregate employment statistics conceal the fact that most of the net employment growth between 1970 and 1992 occurred in the public sector (Diagram 18, panel A). Although common to other countries, this development has been particularly marked in Norway where, in 1991, the Government's share in total employment (about 30 per cent) was more than 50 per cent higher than the average for OECD Europe (Diagram 18, panel B). This occurred at a time when female share in total employment grew substantially (from 31.7 to 45.4 per cent between 1962 and 1992). In addition, because women work fewer hours on average than men, their increasing share in the labour force translated into a decline in average hours worked for the total economy. This demographically driven trend has been accentuated by a secular decline in hours worked by both men and women: women worked 28 per cent fewer hours per year in 1992 as compared with 1962, the corresponding figure for men being 22 per cent. For the economy as a whole, average hours worked fell by 27 per cent over the same period,[29] so that, on an international basis, time Norwegians currently spend at work is less than in any other OECD country for which data are available.[30]

Diagram 19 juxtaposes the employment rate (ER) – the percentage of the working-age population actually employed – and the full-time equivalent employment rate (FTER) – i.e. , the percent of potential hours worked.[31] Despite large increases in the number of individuals employed, the total of hours of work performed has declined more, resulting in a falling FTER.

Both the employment rate and full-time equivalent rate can be expressed as non-employment (NER) or full-time equivalent non-employment rates (FTNER)

Diagram 18. **DISTRIBUTION OF EMPLOYMENT**

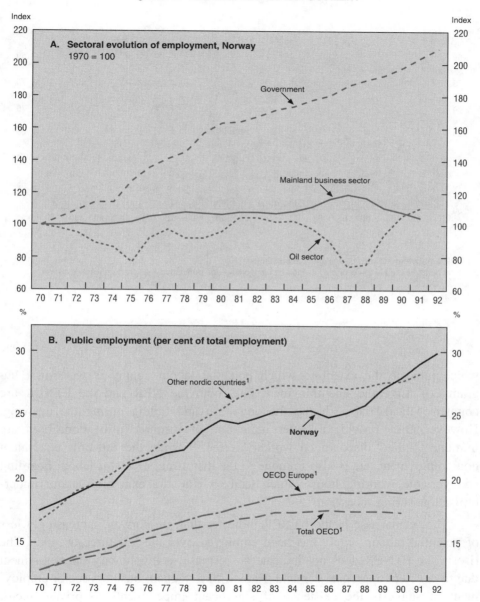

A. **Sectoral evolution of employment, Norway**
1970 = 100

Government

Mainland business sector

Oil sector

B. **Public employment (per cent of total employment)**

Other nordic countries[1]

Norway

OECD Europe[1]

Total OECD[1]

1. Non weighted average.
Source: OECD.

Diagram 19. **EMPLOYMENT RATES**

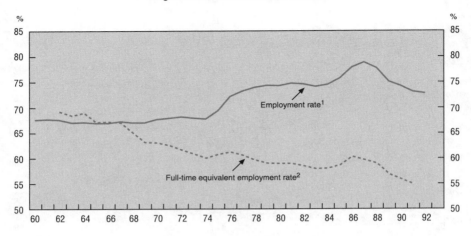

1. Total employment divided by working age population.
2. Total hours worked in the economy divided by the working-age population X 37.5 hours/week X 48 weeks.
Source: OECD.

which indicate the extent to which potential labour supply is working (Diagram 20). Like the unemployment rate, both the NER and the FTNER are counter-cyclical, rising during the downturn and falling during the upswing. However, they provide a better indication of resource utilisation; both are immune to the "discouraged worker" effect,[32] while the full-time equivalent non-employment rate is also immune to the distorting effects of labour hoarding and variable working hours which tend to hide the extent of labour under-utilisation during recessions.

The secular rise in the FTNER indicates that, in Norway, increasingly less of potential labour supply has been employed over the last three decades. The rise in the FTNER does not indicate an increase in involuntary unemployment due to deficient aggregate demand. Rather, like stagnant business sector employment, it suggests the existence of significant impediments to private sector employment growth – operating both on the supply side (declining hours) and the demand side (flat employment).

58

Diagram 20. **ALTERNATIVE MEASURES OF LABOUR UTILISATION**

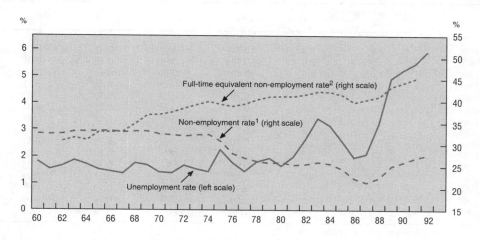

1. 100 – employment rate (see footnote 1 in Diagram 19).
2. 100 – full-time equivalent employment rate (see footnote 2, Diagram 19).
Source: OECD.

Increased duration of unemployment

The rise in unemployment during the 1980s, despite a virtually constant employment rate, is reflected in the increase in the average duration of unemployment spells. It can be analysed in terms of the evolution of the incidence of unemployment (job losing) and the average probability of exit from unemployment (job finding) (Table 13). Although both job losing and job finding have played a role, the rise of unemployment since 1978 is principally due to individuals taking more time to find work. Indeed, between 1978 and 1992, the probability of an unemployed person finding a job within a given month fell from 41 to 18 per cent. This fall in the job finding rate both exceeded the increase in the job losing rate and preceded it by seven years.

Changes in the unemployment rate can be decomposed into impacts due to changes in frequency (more people becoming unemployed from year to year) and duration (each individual spending more time unemployed) (Diagram 21). Increases in duration have accounted for some 70 per cent of the rise in unemployment since 1978. Up until 1987, this was almost entirely due to longer spells

Table 13. **Job finding, job losing and spell duration**

	Unemployment rate	Spell duration [1]	Job losing [2]	Index	Job finding [3]	Index
1978	1.8	2.4	0.74	(100)	0.41	(100)
1979	1.9	2.6	0.73	(99)	0.38	(93)
1980	1.6	2.5	0.66	(89)	0.41	(100)
1981	2.0	2.7	0.75	(101)	0.38	(91)
1982	2.6	3.3	0.79	(107)	0.30	(74)
1983	3.4	3.8	0.88	(119)	0.26	(63)
1984	3.1	4.3	0.73	(99)	0.24	(57)
1985	2.6	3.4	0.77	(104)	0.30	(72)
1986	2.0	2.8	0.70	(95)	0.35	(85)
1987	2.1	3.2	0.64	(86)	0.30	(74)
1988	3.2	3.3	0.96	(130)	0.30	(73)
1989	4.9	4.8	1.02	(138)	0.21	(51)
1990	5.2	5.3	0.98	(132)	0.19	(46)
1991	5.5	5.3	1.03	(139)	0.19	(46)
1992	5.9	5.5	1.08	(146)	0.18	(45)

1. Average unemployment spell duration in months.
2. Steady state probability of becoming unemployed in a given month.
3. Steady state probability of exiting unemployment in a given month.
Source: OECD calculations from data supplied by the Norwegian Ministry of Finance.

Diagram 21. **IMPACT OF FREQUENCY AND DURATION
ON THE UNEMPLOYMENT RATE**

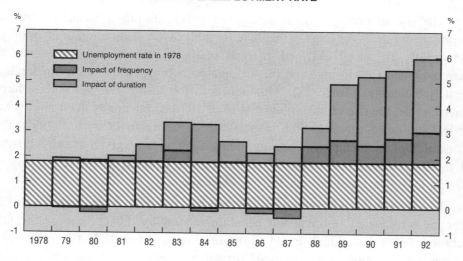

Source: Norwegian Central Bureau of Statistics.

60

of unemployment. In fact, during certain periods (1979-81, 1984-87), unemployment was higher than in 1978 even though the impact of changes in the frequency of unemployment was either zero or negative.

Higher concentration of unemployment

With the rise in the average duration of unemployment, long-term unemployment (LTU) has increased both in absolute terms and as a percentage of all unemployed (Diagram 22, panel A). While, prior to 1989, Norway regularly had the lowest long-term unemployment in the OECD area, now fully one-third of OECD countries (including a number of those with much higher unemployment rates) are doing better in this regard (*OECD Employment Outlook,* 1993). This deterioration in relative performance is in fact probably understated since the size of active labour market policies in Norway (see below) tends to interrupt artificially unemployment spells. It must be stressed, however, that Norway entered into recession two to three years before most other European countries, which may partly explain why long-term unemployment increased more rapidly there than elsewhere.

In addition to the increased share of long-term unemployed, the concentration of unemployment among certain classes of workers seems to have intensified. Unemployment is particularly concentrated among low educated people, a phenomena which has tended to increase over time (Diagram 22, panel B). As in other OECD countries, unemployment is also very concentrated among young workers (Diagram 22, panel C), this in spite of programmes which guarantee youths under the age of twenty either a job or a position in a training programme. In fact, it is young males with little formal education who are bearing the brunt of unemployment in the current recession (Table 14). The difference between less well educated youth[33] and older workers and their contemporaries with an upper secondary education is particularly marked. Both among youths and older workers, those with compulsory education have an unemployment rate about 50 per cent higher than those with upper secondary schooling. In contrast, the difference for young prime age males is much less pronounced. Among females the pattern is slightly different: there it is prime age females with low educational whose unemployment rate is more than twice that of their better educated peers, probably reflecting the concentration of labour market newcomers within this group.

Diagram 22. **CONCENTRATION OF UNEMPLOYMENT**

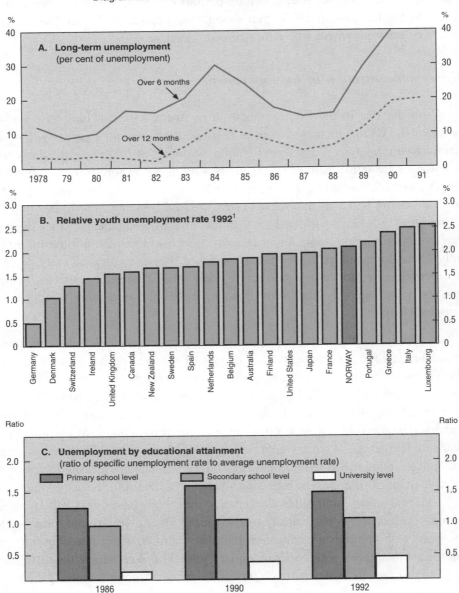

1. Youth unemployment rate (below 25 years of age) compared to overall unemployment rate.
Sources: Norwegian Central Bureau of Statistics; OECD.

Table 14. **Unemployment rates by educational attainment and sex, 1992**

Education level	Males				Females			
	All	20-24	25-39	40-54	All	20-24	25-39	40-54
Compulsory	10.0	30.8	5.5	7.7	7.5	14.3	11.8	3.5
Upper secondary	6.7	20.5	5.0	4.4	5.9	10.3	5.0	3.0
Higher education	3.0	18.8	0.8	1.7	2.5	10.0	2.5	1.3
Total	6.5	23.0	4.0	4.0	5.2	11.1	5.1	2.9

Source: Bank of Norway.

Because of the discouraged worker effect and an expansion of educational measures, Table 14 understates the degree of concentration of unemployment observed among unskilled older and younger workers. Indeed, it is precisely these groups whose participation rates have fallen the most during the recession. To illustrate this aspect, the upper panel of Table 15 shows the falls in the employment and participation rates sustained by different age/sex categories between the employment peak of 1987 and 1992. The lower panel makes much the same calculation, comparing current employment and participation rates with their averages from the period (1980-1984) prior to the employment boom.

Table 15. **Changes in employment and participation rates**
Per cent

Ages	Period: 1987-1992			
	Males		Females	
	Employment	Participation	Employment	Participation
16 to 19	−34.06	−25.90	−37.39	−31.72
20 to 24	−21.63	−11.16	−12.75	−7.10
25 to 29	−7.75	−3.69	−6.36	−1.35
60 plus	−24.31	−23.03	−15.04	−13.74
	Period: 1980-84-1992			
16 to 19	−24.78	−18.88	−17.55	−12.47
20 to 24	−17.68	−8.22	−3.71	2.52
25 to 59	−6.82	−3.14	6.04	10.88
60 plus	−33.0	−31.55	−14.14	−13.46

Source: OECD.

Such evidence confirms that job losses were concentrated among young and older workers: over 33 per cent of the positions held by young men and 25 per cent of the positions held by older men disappeared between 1987 and 1992. For women the employment losses were smaller except for the youngest age group. The full extent of these losses is not reflected in unemployment data because these same groups also had the largest falls in participation rates. This pattern of concentrated job losses is not an artifact of the 1985-1987 employment boom, however. A similar pattern is observed by comparing average employment and participation between 1980 and 1985 with their levels in 1992, the principle difference being that more young adult and prime age female workers are now participating and that more prime age females are employed than before the employment boom.

The role of institutions and policies

Wage determination

This subsection discusses the extent to which Norwegian wage setting institutions have been able to deliver aggregate and relative wage flexibility. Indications are that although aggregate real wages can be significantly flexible, they have not responded sufficiently to the enduring labour market slack of the recent recession and that a compressed wage structure might have reduced employment opportunities for low-skilled workers.

As described in detail in the 1988/89 OECD *Economic Survey*, the Norwegian wage formation process is based on a two tier system whereby a central wage agreement is concluded between the employer's organisation, the NHO and the principle labour organisation, the LO, which represents approximately one-half of the 57 per cent of the labour force that is unionised. Traditionally this agreement, which may contain a minimum or a general wage increase, has a significant impact on wage negotiation between other labour market organisations and, to some extent also, on the non-unionised sector. Although the precise form of the wage agreement changes from year to year, reflecting the evolving concerns of labour market partners, there is normally provision for firm or sector level negotiations which – taking the central offer as a departure point – can expand or fall away from it depending on local conditions.

Diagram 23. **WAGE DEVELOPMENTS**
Mainland business sector

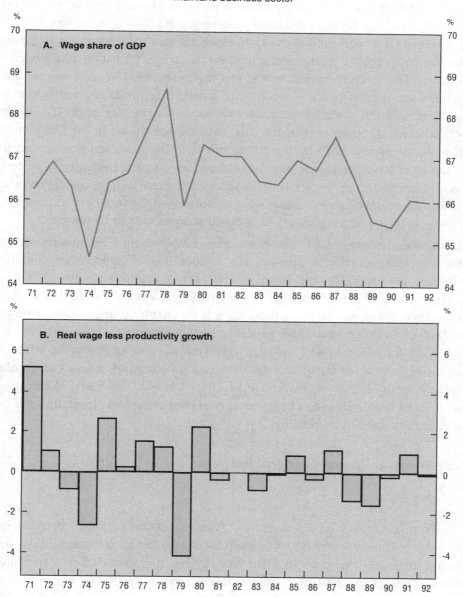

Source: OECD.

65

In recent years, there has been considerable flexibility incorporated into the local level with provisions for no increase and even absolute falls in wage levels. Nevertheless, after falling substantially in the second half of the 1980s, the share of wages in GDP recovered in the early 1990s (Diagram 23, panel A), suggesting that the influence of rising unemployment on wage formation has tended to decrease. This is corroborated by the fact that, over 1990-92, real wages in the business sector grew in line or even more rapidly than productivity,[34] despite the rapid deterioration of the labour market situation (Diagram 23, panel B). One has to bear in mind, however, that the real wage figures shown in the Diagram are gross wage costs deflated by the output prices of the Mainland business sector. As the latter have been weak in most recent years – particularly for raw material based manufacturing – profits have been squeezed despite moderate wage growth. Such developments have led the Norwegian Government to co-operate actively with the social partners in order to achieve cuts in labour costs.

Studies undertaken by The Norwegian Employment Commission indicate that wage differentials in Norway are smaller than in most other countries, implying that low-skill workers are in a weaker competitive position than those of higher skill. The concentration of unemployment among low-skilled workers, as outlined above, suggest that these have been unable to price themselves into the market. In this regard, there appear to be indications of a bias in the Norwegian wage formation system towards wage compression. In particular, while the central agreement, or tariff, sets the increases for low wage earners in absolute nominal terms, higher wages are fixed on an *ad valorem* basis. Whereas the increases of high earners can be under or over shot at the local level, those of low wage earners tend to be binding.

Labour market support programmes

Overview

From an international perspective, Norway's efforts on behalf of the unemployed are at once extensive and generous and go far in favouring active over passive measures. In terms of GDP Norway has the sixth highest expenditure programmes within the OECD despite having one of the lowest unemployment rates (Table 16). Measured as a share of GDP per percentage point of unemployment, Norway has the third highest expenditure rate.

Table 16. **Expenditures on labour market programmes, 1992**

	ALMP as a per cent of GDP [1]	Rank	ALMP/ (ALMP + PLMP) [2]	Rank
Norway	**1.14**	**6**	**43.02**	**5**
Australia	0.34	17	16.27	19
Austria	0.30	19	20.55	17
Belgium	1.04	7	26.87	13
Canada	0.68	11	22.97	16
Denmark	1.56	4	23.89	15
Finland	1.76	2	31.88	10
France	0.80	9	28.37	11
Germany	1.64	3	47.40	4
Greece	0.39	15	17.11	18
Ireland	1.51	5	34.32	8
Italy	0.00	21	0.00	21
Japan	0.32	18	71.11	1
Netherlands	1.04	7	32.30	9
New Zealand	0.74	10	27.61	12
Portugal	0.63	12	60.00	2
Spain	0.57	14	15.62	20
Sweden	3.21	1	53.59	3
Switzerland	0.27	20	42.86	6
United Kingdom	0.59	13	25.88	14
United States	0.35	16	41.67	7

1. Active Labour Market Programmes as a percent of GDP.
2. Expenditures on Active Labour Market Programmes as a share of total Labour Market Programme expenditures (Active and Passive Labour Market Programmes).
Source: OECD Employment Outlook, 1993

High programme expenditures need not, however, imply effective labour market policies. During the last two decades, the unemployment insurance scheme has been repeatedly extended to the point that, in conjunction with various active labour market programmes (ALMP), it is possible for an unemployed worker to receive between 60 and 40 per cent of his working salary for as much as six years without ever getting an unsubsidised job. This has most likely played a role in the increase in unemployment duration observed since 1978. At the same time Norway's ALMP expanded dramatically: between 1988 and 1993 participation in such programmes rose by 53 000 (or 3 per cent of the labour force). In addition, though approximately in line with European standards,[35] Norway's job protection legislation (JPL) has also probably lowered overall employment levels and reduced the labour market's margin of flexibility. The paragraphs below discuss in more detail the characteristics of these different programmes and their drawbacks.

Unemployment insurance system

Almost all OECD countries have put into place systems of unemployment insurance providing temporary income support to help unemployed individuals bridge the gap between jobs. All such systems involve a conflict between the desire to ease transitions to new jobs and the disincentive effects inherent in providing individuals with financial assistance when not working. In the light of evidence in OECD countries,[36] at least two features are critical to the unemployment insurance system's impact on the duration of spells and the overall unemployment rate – the first being the replacement rate (a measure of the percentage of labour income replaced by benefits) and the second the maximum duration of unemployment benefits. Effective benefit duration in Norway is long, as indicated in the box below. An unemployed person is permitted to refuse up to three suitable job offers in every 12 month period with only temporary suspensions of benefits, while, as indicated above, the maximum duration of the system now makes possible, in conjunction with ALMP, virtually indefinite benefits.

Perhaps, not coincidentally, it is also the case that a pronounced asymmetry in labour supply has been developed. Table 17 contrasts labour force and employment growth in 1977-84, 1985-87, 1988-89 and 1990-93 which correspond to periods before, during and after the 1985-86 demand boom. Whereas employment and labour force growth moved more or less in step during the expansion of 1985-87, the labour force fell at a very slow and constant rate after the employment boom was over.[37] It may be that the duration of unemployment insurance slowed labour force withdrawal.

Although it may offer an alternative to lay-offs, the generous treatment of the "partly" unemployed (those working involuntarily reduced hours) prior to April 1993 may have contributed to the decline in hours supplied. In particular, an individual who agreed to work one day less per week could receive up to 93 per cent of normal salary while enjoying a long weekend every week for a period of over $7\frac{1}{2}$ years.[38] With the newly reformed system, the maximum benefit duration for the partially unemployed is now the same as for the fully unemployed and, in order to qualify for benefit, one must be at least 40 per cent unemployed. However, the system remains relatively generous by international standards and lacks sufficiently enforceable job-search requirements.

While the work disincentive effects of unemployment insurance in the example described above are patent, they are equally important in less extreme

68

Unemployment insurance

Major reforms:

1971: Maximum duration 21 weeks per "benefit year".
1975: Maximum duration 40 weeks per calendar year.
1984: Maximum duration 80 weeks with a minimum of 26 weeks between spells.
1990: Calculation of eligibility period based on continuous time not calendar year.
1991: Ineligibility period reduced to 13 weeks.
1992: Ineligibility period waived if no ALMP or educational programmes offered.

Benefit qualification:

- Available to any worker, willing to work at going wages, who has earned 75 per cent of the basic amount in the last calendar year or on average over the last three calendar years.
- Available to "partially" unemployed – those who have experienced a 40 per cent reduction in hours worked.

Facts:

- 100 per cent state financed – no employee or employer premia.
- Three-day waiting period before benefits begin (second most generous system in the OECD, nine countries require no waiting period), four weeks if a voluntary quit (second most generous system in the OECD; only the Netherlands has a more generous system).
- As indicated above, duration is now limited to 80 weeks but 93 weeks in cases where the ineligibility period of 13 weeks is waived. If the qualification condition mentioned above is still fulfilled, a new period of 93 weeks may be granted. Workers are almost guaranteed an ALMP when benefits expire which then re-qualifies them for unemployment insurance.
- One of the highest replacement ratios in the OECD (62 per cent)

Recent reforms:

- Tightened access to benefits for the partially unemployed, who now must experience a 40 per cent reduction in weekly hours to qualify and whose benefit duration is the same as for a fully unemployed worker. Prior to April 1993, a 20 per cent fall in weekly hours qualified a worker for benefits and maximum duration of benefits varied inversely with the degree of unemployment. Thus a person experiencing 20 per cent unemployment would have access to benefits for five times as long as a fully unemployed person – the krone value of benefits received by each being the same.

(continued on next page)

(continued)

- Increased sanctions for those who refuse suitable employment. Every time an individual refuses a suitable job his access to benefits can be temporarily suspended (8 weeks after the first refusal and 12 weeks after the second), after three refusals within a period of 12 months benefits can be suspended for six months. Previously benefits could be suspended for a maximum of 12 weeks.
- The overall functioning of the unemployed insurance system is currently being reviewed.

cases, such as unemployed workers who, when offered a job at average or below average wages, retain as little as 20 to 25 per cent of their salary once benefit withdrawals and taxes are accounted for. Diagram 24 illustrates such work disincentive effects by showing the probability that an employed person will accept a job (or leave the labour force) – the exit rate – as his/her unemployment spell lengthens. It points out that job findings increase markedly as benefits expire. The importance of the exit rate as an indicator of the unemployment insurance system's disincentive effects is attenuated, however, by the fact that a large percentage of the increase in transitions is explained by various active labour market programmes which guarantee jobs to those whose benefits expire. Nevertheless, a similar jump in the hazard rate at the point of benefit exhaustion has been observed in other OECD countries (Canada, the United States, Japan

Table 17. **Employment and labour force growth,
pre and post the 1985-86 demand boom**

Percentage change, annual compound rates

	Employment growth	Labour force growth
1977 to 1984	0.91	1.16
1985 to 1987	2.75	2.47
1988 to 1989	−1.85	−0.37
1990 to 1993[1]	−0.35	0.2

1. 1993 figure is an average of the first three quarters.
Source: OECD.

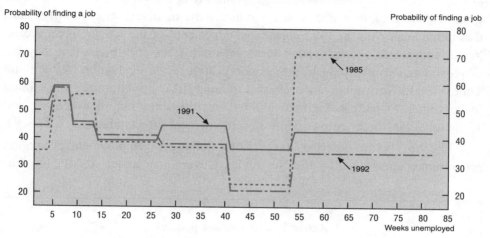

Diagram 24. **JOB FINDING PROBABILITIES**[1]

1. The probability of finding a job in the indicated week of an unemployment spell. This is based on the distribution of unemployment spells assuming a steady state and that the hazard each week in this period is equal to the period average.
Sources: Norwegian Central Bureau of Statistics; OECD.

and France) and is robust to differences in age, sex, occupation and other variables.[39]

Active labour market policies

Compared with passive income support schemes (such as unemployment insurance), active labour market policies (ALMP) present the advantage of strengthening the potential for employability of participating workers. By improving the matching process and upgrading skill levels, they may reduce structural unemployment and thereby contain wage pressure. However, by reducing registered unemployment, they may at the same time put upward pressure on wages. Their effects are thus highly dependent upon the extent to which relevant skills are actually upgraded, or at least maintained, through participation in such programmes.[40] Cross-sectional macroeconomic estimates reported in OECD *Employment Outlook*, (1993) and Layard, Nickell and Jackman (1992) suggest that, in Norway, the beneficial effects of ALMP do outweigh the negative impacts. A separate set of calculations presented in the first of these publications indicates that ALMP in Norway may be responsible for lowering the long-term unemployment rate by 2.5 percentage points. It is not clear, however, to what extent ALMP actually reduce economic inactivity. Involvement in ALMP means that individuals, who in 1993 constituted 3 per cent of the labour force, are no longer counted as unemployed – but it does not necessarily mean that they are employed and contributing to the economy. In a recent evaluation (Raaum and Thorp, 1993), Norwegian labour market training (LMT) programmes were found to contribute to increased employability over the short run (between six and 12 months) but there are no significant employment effects after 12 months.[41]

The box below describes the various training or employment promotion programmes undertaken by the Norwegian Government under ALMP. In addi-

---

Active labour market policies

Facts:

- ALMP spending as percent of GDP was 1.14 per cent in 1992 (the sixth highest in OECD).
- Ratio of ALMP expenditures to all labour market expenditures was 43 per cent (the fifth highest in OECD).
- As of 1987 all youth (under 20) are guaranteed a job, a position in an ALMP or a place in school.

Programmes:

- *SKAP:* a public sector employment measure whereby the central government funds jobs at the municipal and district level which are made available to long-term unemployed workers whose unemployment insurance has or is about to expire.
- *Wage subsidies* in the amount of 50 per cent are made available both to private and public sector firms and are provided to individuals experiencing long spells of unemployment or members of high risk groups: youth and older workers among others.
- *Educational support* programmes and access to some form of schooling or a place in a labour market scheme is guaranteed to all individuals under 20.
- *Training* programmes take several forms, including one aimed at labour market entrants which lasts for six to ten months and involves a combination of formal and on-the-job training; training is provided both within the traditional education system and by the private sector.
- *Substitute schemes* is a new programme which seeks to encourage employed workers to upgrade their skills and provides firms with unemployed workers to temporarily replace the employee on training.
- *Rehabilitation measures* include a number of programmes aimed at improving the employability of handicapped labour market participants.

Table 18. **Active labour market programmes**
May 1993

	Enrolment	Per cent of labour force
Public sector employment measures	15 516	0.73
SKAP (job creation in municipalities)	14 052	0.66
Wage subsidies	2 606	0.12
Qualification measures	39 976	1.89
Labour market training courses	26 069	1.23
Trainee places	13 907	0.66
Sabbatical substitutes	2 459	0.12
Sub-total	61 557	2.91
Rehabilitation measures	13 687	0.65
Total	76 224	3.60

Sources: Ministry of Labour and OECD.

tion, Table 18 gives an indication of the size of each of these programmes both in absolute terms and expressed as a percentage of the labour force. It clearly shows that ALMPs in Norway are extensive. By far the largest category of programmes corresponds to measures explicitly designed to upgrade unemployed worker's skills. The second largest category concerns public sector employment programmes aimed at breaking up long spells of unemployment and at preventing the erosion of labour market skills.

Disability insurance

In Norway, as in certain other countries, the disability pension system has, to some extent, been used to provide income support to unemployed workers; medical illness has not been a necessary eligibility condition in this system. The correlation between labour market conditions and the rate of inflow into disability pensions is striking: between 1975 and 1992 the number of pension recipients increased from 156 000 to some 236 000 or from 5.6 to 8.4 per cent of the working age population.[42] Those who have been granted disability pensions that way cease to exercise an influence on wage bargaining and thus weaken the adjustment of wages following cyclical and structural shocks. Some estimates suggest that, since 1975, as much as 67 per cent of the increase in disability pensioners is for reasons other than strictly medical.

The dashed line in Diagram 25 indicates what the unemployment rate would be if those people receiving disability pensions for non-medical reasons were considered labour force participants and unemployed. This adjusted measure suggests that Norway's disability programme causes the unemployment rate to understate inactivity by as much as 2.2 percentage points. Judging from the thick solid line in the Diagram – which combines both non-medical disability pensions and ALMP participants with the unemployed – as much as 10 to 11 per cent of the potential labour force may actually be regarded as economically inactive.

Recent reforms (see box) have made access to disability pensions much more difficult, notably by requiring second opinions from neutral physicians and by strengthening the medical criteria when evaluating eligibility. Such reforms seem already to have been reflected both in the number of applicants and of pensions granted, which fell in 1992. In addition, from 1993, certain cases of previously granted pensions are being re-examined, in particular with regard to younger persons, with the aim of securing re-entry into the labour market.

Diagram 25. **UNEMPLOYMENT ADJUSTED
FOR EFFECTIVE LABOUR SUPPLY**

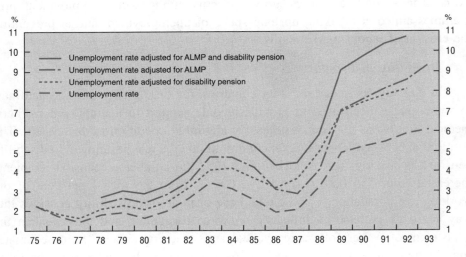

Legend:
— Unemployment rate adjusted for ALMP and disability pension
–·– Unemployment rate adjusted for ALMP
····· Unemployment rate adjusted for disability pension
– – Unemployment rate

Sources: Norwegian Central Bureau of Statistics; OECD.

Job protection legislation

Job protection legislation (JPL) is generally concerned with "hiring and firing" rules governing *inter alia* unfair dismissals, length of employment contracts, lay-offs for economic reasons, severance payments, minimum notice periods and prior consultation with labour representatives. For firms wishing, for technical reasons, to retain a particularly qualified manpower, such rules may add to efficiency, for example by encouraging increased investment in human capital and by reducing contracting costs. For other companies, JPL rules – in particular those applying to restrictions of dismissals and firms ability to hire temporary workers (see box) – may, on the other hand, contribute to reduce employment opportunities. In any case, it must be stressed that, in the absence of a

Job protection legislation

Facts:

- The provisions of at least three acts come under the general rubric of Job Protection Legislation (JPL):
- The *Work Environment Act* (WEA) includes provisions regulating working time, appointments, layoffs and dismissals. It requires firms to transfer workers, if possible, from one position to another in cases of illness, injury or layoff. The act includes the workers' right to remain at a job until a court verdict is reached in cases where the worker challenges his dismissal.
- The *Employment Act* (EA) grants the State a monopoly on job placement services and prohibits hiring out except in selected sectors.
- The *Act on Obligatory Pay* (AOP) regulates temporary layoffs.

Specific rules:

- Prohibition against unwarranted dismissal (WEA): workers can be dismissed for warranted reasons such as curtailed operations or rationalisations but may not if the employer has other suitable work to offer. For rationalisations, the needs of the enterprise are weighed against those of the inconvenience to the employee –with the practical result that some rationalisations are deemed unwarranted and dismissals disallowed.
- Right to remain in position (WEA): implies that a worker who contests the reasons given for his dismissal has the right to keep his job until such time as the courts decide his case. The court may require the employee to leave if it finds it unreasonable that employment should continue – where factors such as the size of the firm and the nature of the dispute are used to determine "reasonableness".
- Restrictions on hours worked and overtime pay (WEA):
- Prohibition of fixed term contracts (WEA): these are illegal under the provisions of the right to remain in position legislation as they allow a firm to let a contract lapse effectively dismissing a worker without cause. The only exception to this is where there exists a well defined job of fixed duration, such as traineeships, short-term replacement contracts or work related to active labour market measures.
- Prohibition on private employment agencies and hiring out (EAHO). EAHO are in principle not allowed under Norwegian legislation. General exemptions are given though for secretarial work and some other minor sectors. In addition, firms can apply for derogations.
- Payments to temporarily laid off workers are for 3 days at full pay (AOP), followed by up to 52 weeks, 26 weeks until 1 January 1994, of unemployment benefits.
- In May 1993, a legislation was adopted granting foreigners from EEA countries, and working in Norway, employment terms equal to Norwegian workers. Effec-

(continued on next page)

(continued)

> tive from 1 January 1994, this legislation institutes a board that shall deal with allegations of so-called "social dumping" (this means that labour market organisations to a large extent can enforce collective agreements upon all employees and employers within a branch or geographical area). Such regulation may have the practical effect of requiring non-unionised Norwegian firms to adopt the unionised sector's wage and benefit agreements because of non-discriminatory provisions in the EFTA.

specific legislation, the private sector always has the possibility to adopt employment protection practices if needed.

Although it is not the intent of Norwegian lay-off provisions to prevent firms from making adjustments which are economically necessary, they may, by sufficiently raising the cost of dismissal, discourage new hiring.[43] Though relatively few dismissals are challenged, the actual number almost certainly understates the economic influence of the legislation. In practice, firms seek to avoid border-line dismissals or are forced to provide dismissal packages which are sufficiently generous as to preclude court challenges. Moreover, restrictions on short-term hiring reduce firms' flexibility when faced with fluctuations in demand and raise the costs of hiring labour of uncertain quality – such as new entrants. As a result, overall employment levels tend to be lower than they would be otherwise and job opportunities for new entrants especially scarce. This dynamic is perhaps reflected in the fact that employment in construction and manufacturing fell by 7.5 per cent from 1989 to 1990 while, over the same period, overtime hours in these industries increased from about 2.5 to 4.5 per cent of total hours.

Prospects for reform

A number of proposals aimed at enhancing employment opportunities and improving labour market flexibility have already been put forward in the August 1992 report of the *Norwegian Employment Commission* (NEC). In addition, the

Government has convened a new commission to look into youth wages which is expected to finish its deliberations early in 1994. The paragraphs below briefly review the proposals already made and discuss the scope for possible further action.

Recent initiatives: the "solidarity alternative"

The principal recommendations of the NEC, presented as a "*solidarity alternative*", include a programme of aggregate wage moderation aimed at reducing unit labour costs by 10 per cent (see above), a programme of public expenditure restraint which would limit Government expenditures to the rate of growth of Mainland GDP, a review of expenditures designed to rely less on transfers (especially as concerns employment measures), a number of programmes aimed at promoting employment in the short run (including one for local infrastructure investment), as well as policy reforms aimed at reducing impediments to employment growth.

Among the latter, the NEC recommended that a number of job protection provisions be re-evaluated especially insofar as they impede the successful insertion of new entrants' into the labour force. Specifically the suggestion was that more liberal regulations with respect to short-term contracts, hiring out and private employment agencies be introduced at least temporarily. The commission underlined the importance of tight job search provisions and effective enforcement, and that unemployment benefits and duration should not be so generous as to remove work incentives. In addition, a review of the financing of unemployment benefits was suggested and it was recognised that efforts should be directed at reducing absenteeism due to alleged illness. Finally, while calling for a strengthening of active labour market measures (a recommendation already followed up), the NEC also suggested that such measures could be made more effective if those workers most likely to be aided that way were targeted more closely.

A number of proposals by the NEC have already been endorsed in the Government's latest long-term programme, including: a policy of wage restraint, the moderation of Government expenditure growth, the re-allocation of some NKr 5 billion of expenditure from transfers towards investment, several education and employment measures. The 1994 Budget contains further initiatives to reduce youth unemployment and improve job relevant skills, including an exten-

78

sion of the guarantee that youth under 20 years be provided with either a job or an educational opportunity. In particular, the Government strengthened apprenticeship schemes by providing additional subsidies to firms that employ apprentices.

Scope for further action

The preceding review of Norwegian labour market conditions suggests that certain labour market institutions and policies (specifically: the unemployment insurance system, some features of ALMPs, job protection legislation, the disability pension system and the lack of relative wage flexibility) may have impeded the adjustment process in Norway resulting in increased unemployment duration. To counteract these developments, access to the unemployment insurance system should be tightened and the maximum duration of benefits should be reduced. In addition, there is a conflict between the employability enhancing features of ALMPs (which were increased by another 6 per cent in the latest budget) and the work disincentives they share with passive measures. Given the large sums of money currently devoted to ALMP – about 3.7 per cent of state non-oil revenues – and the equivocal evidence as to their effectiveness, a thorough review of their relative costs and benefits seems to be in order.

At the same time, restrictions on short-term employment contracts and hiring out should be eased. Experience in other OECD countries which allow for fixed-term contracts and temporary workers suggest indeed that most successful moves from unemployment to employment involve some form of temporary or fixed-term contract (*OECD Employment Outlook,* 1993). Based upon market needs, such contracts may contribute to reduce youth unemployment and prepare the ground for full-time employment opportunities. More generally, the Government should use its influence in the wage formation process to encourage a better consistency between real wages and productivity levels while using the tax system to promote distributional issues.

IV. Conclusions

The Norwegian economy is recovering slowly from the prolonged recession of the late 1980s and early 1990s. Initially relying heavily on rising oil investment and public expenditure, the upturn has recently become more broadly based, as private consumption picked up after a long period of consolidation of households' financial position. The revival of private demand is still fragile, however, as evidenced by the cautious attitude of consumers in the first half of 1993 and the persistent sluggishness of Mainland business investment. Helped by a significant expansion of active labour market programmes, the unemployment rate has stabilised, though at a relatively high level (6 per cent) by Norwegian standards. With wage pressures subsiding, inflation has remained remarkably low despite indirect tax increases and the small exchange-rate depreciation following the floating of the krone in December 1992. While contributing to boost Norway's international competitiveness, these developments have not yet been reflected in any significant improvement in export performance of "traditional" industries. By contrast, oil and gas exports have remained buoyant, allowing the maintenance of a sizeable current account surplus and a rapid reduction in net foreign indebtedness.

Improving economic fundamentals, easier monetary conditions and progress in the private sector's financial consolidation have paved the way for a self-sustained recovery: real GDP growth is projected to strengthen progressively to reach, on average, more than 3 per cent in 1994 and nearly 4 per cent in 1995; this implies $2\frac{1}{4}$ and 3 per cent growth, respectively for Mainland activity. Some decline in the household saving ratio should help sustain private consumption, which, in turn, could lead to a revival of business investment. By boosting non-oil exports, the expected pick-up in world trade should also provide impetus to growth. Nonetheless, unemployment is expected to decline only slightly, as increased employment opportunities associated with the recovery are likely to be

80

reflected in some cyclical rebound of labour-force participation rates. Given continued slack in product and labour markets, inflation should remain moderate, thereby creating room for further improvement in international competitiveness. As a result, with rising oil production expected to continue, Norway's external surplus is likely to grow further. These projections are subject to major uncertainties, however, especially with regard to the world recovery, as Norwegian export revenues are highly sensitive to both cyclical and commodity price developments. On the domestic side, uncertainty remains as to whether the ongoing financial consolidation process is actually coming to an end and whether, as a result, consumers will be induced to resume more normal spending behaviour.

Given these uncertainties, keeping interest rates low appears crucial to sustain demand and confidence in the private sector. With a return to more stable foreign exchange-market conditions, the monetary authorities have been able to reduce short rates gradually to below those prevailing elsewhere in Europe. The decision to let the krone float has not undermined the credibility of monetary policy obtained during the fixed exchange rate regime. This is evidenced in the substantial decline in long-term interest rates and the inflow of foreign capital, which has allowed a rapid rebuilding of foreign exchange reserves. Consolidating these gains will require that the orientation of monetary policy continues to be clearly perceived by the market and the general public. While monetary authorities still regard the maintenance of exchange rate stability as essential, they realise that a return to a formal fixed exchange rate arrangement may take some time. Therefore, the question could be raised whether a more explicit nominal anchor for monetary policy – such as, among others, inflation targets – might help to signal the authorities' resolve to keep inflation under control.

There is also a need for change in the mix of monetary and fiscal instruments in the future. In 1993 fiscal policy continued the expansionary stance initiated in the late 1980s. While the general government deficit remained below 3 per cent of GDP, the central government budget position, adjusted for oil, deteriorated further. This deterioration was due primarily to rapidly rising transfers and labour-market measures, as well as, to a lesser extent, some reduction in the tax burden. Some tightening of the fiscal stance was decided in the 1994 Budget, which aims at containing the growth in public spending substantially below that of GDP. However, medium-term budget projections suggest that, by 1997, the overall deficit will have fallen – in terms of GDP – only little from the current level despite a continued increased in net oil revenue. This will imply a continued erosion of the government's currently comfortable net asset position.

A more ambitious medium-term budget consolidation strategy would thus be desirable for at least three reasons. *First*, it is important to preserve financial market confidence and ensure that monetary conditions remain supportive of the authorities' objective of revitalising the Mainland economy. *Second*, with continued deficits, there is a risk of substantial fiscal adjustment problems in the event of an adverse oil-price shock and, in any case, when oil revenue tapers off. *Third*, as emphasised in previous Surveys, the way oil wealth is used should take into account inter-generational equity considerations. Indeed, generational accounting estimates suggest that the tax burden would have to increase in the future unless a share of oil income is set aside (*e.g.* in the "Petroleum Fund" established in 1991).

In these conditions, continuous structural reform aimed at improving the functioning of the economy appears all the more important to achieve higher output and employment growth in the coming years. Following the liberalisation of financial markets in the 1980s, major reforms have been introduced to this effect in the fields of taxation, environment and the energy sector. Subsequent structural initiatives have been mainly related to the implementation of the European Economic Area agreement, which has important implications for trade and competition policies. Areas where additional reform would seem essential include agriculture, the public sector, banking and the labour market.

There is a clear need for reducing the present level of *agricultural support* – one of the highest among OECD countries – as it implies that social objectives are currently achieved at an excessive cost to the Norwegian economy. Empirical evidence indicates that policy goals such as self-sufficiency and the preservation of population levels in distant regions could be obtained with significantly lower use of resources (about one-half of actual agricultural employment). Potential efficiency gains in the *public sector* (which raised its share in total employment from 23 per cent in 1980 to almost 30 per cent in 1992) also seem to be substantial, notably in the areas of health and education. As for *banks*, the challenge now facing the authorities, after the management of the crisis, is to create the conditions for restoring a profitable banking industry. Progress has been made in this direction recently, as reflected in the overall improvement of banks' balance sheets. Further action would be necessary, however, to ensure a healthy and competitive financial system. This would require both some further rationalisation of the existing banking structure (including traditional State banks' activities) and the pursuit of the gradual return of banks' capital to private ownership, which has started recently.

Labour market reform is also becoming of primary importance. While Norway's employment performance has been outstanding for much of the last three decades, it has deteriorated markedly in recent years. This appears to reflect more than a cyclical increase in unemployment. Indeed, symptoms of rising non-cyclical unemployment were visible before the oil-related collapse of demand in the mid-1980s, suggesting the existence of structural deficiencies in the labour market. In addition, institutional and policy features of the Norwegian labour market may have affected the economy's ability to adapt to external shocks. Recognising such drawbacks, the "National Employment Commission" (NEC), appointed in 1991 to develop an overall employment strategy, proposed a pro-tracted period of wage restraint coupled with structural measures – including a reorientation of public expenditure from income transfers to training and other active labour-market programmes – in order to reduce the rising level of unemployment.

Although NEC recommendations have been largely reflected in recent budg-ets, there remains ample scope for improving the functioning of the labour market. In particular, a better consistency between wage and productivity levels should be encouraged. It is also important to ease the integration of unemployed unskilled workers and youth into the labour market. Recent policy initiatives, including skill-focused active labour market programmes (ALMP) and increased educational opportunities, should support such integration. More generally, the tightening of eligibility provisions should be pursued – for instance in the area of disability pensions – in order to free resources for active labour-market measures, whose efficiency should be subject to permanent scrutiny. The duration of unem-ployment insurance, especially as it interacts with ALMP, should be reduced, and job search requirements should be more strictly enforced. Finally, as suggested by the NEC, steps should be taken to relax the restrictions on the possibilities to hire labour on a temporary basis.

In summary, despite uncertainties about the profile of the emerging eco-nomic upturn, the fundamental conditions appear to be in place for sustained growth of the Norwegian economy. Inflation has fallen markedly and the external position has improved considerably. The process of financial consolidation, which started earlier in Norway than in other countries, seems near completion, and monetary conditions have eased substantially since the floating of the krone. However, economic growth over the next few years is unlikely to prove sufficient to make major inroads into relatively high unemployment. This highlights the need for more intensive labour-market reform, the more so since employment growth can no longer be pursued by means of additional fiscal stimulus and creation of public sector jobs. In fact, substantial fiscal tightening is required, as the present budgetary stance is clearly not sustainable. Such changes in fiscal and labour market policies would need to be supplemented by further structural initiatives – in particular in agriculture, banking and the public sector – in order to make the economy more efficient and enhance its ability to adapt to the evolving domestic and international environment.

Notes and references

1. Oil investment is measured on an "accrual" basis, *i.e.* platforms under construction are included.

2. The conversion of the Directorate of Public Construction and Property from a government agency to a public corporation implies that investments carried out by this institution are no longer counted as "government investment" in the national accounts.

3. See OECD *Economic Survey of Norway*, 1990/91.

4. According to some estimates, the changes implied by the adoption of the State Budget for 1993, and in particular the increase in the general VAT rate, would tend to increase consumer prices by 0.4 to 0.7 percentage points.

5. Anticipating a change from net debt to net credit in the banks' net position with the central bank, the Bank of Norway altered its mode of operation in June 1993 by letting the banks' deposit rate become the floor rate and the overnight lending rate (the "D-rate") the ceiling for money market rates. Prior to June the D-rate had been the floor.

6. When assessing recent trends in bank profitability, the low-rate deposits of NKr 15 billion which the central bank has placed with commercial and savings banks need to be taken into account. As these boosted banks' net interest income, their operating results were directly affected. The Ministry of Finance has estimated, based on the difference between the deposit rate of 2 per cent and the six-month money market rate (chosen as benchmark), that such deposits represented a subsidy to the banking system of more than NKr 1 billion in both 1992 and 1993. This is the equivalent of 10 to 15 per cent of banks' net interest earnings. However, this factor does not alter the conclusion that there has been an underlying improvement in banks' balance sheets since 1992.

7. In addition, broad money supply was significantly affected by the release of tax-subsidised saving (SMS) deposits in September 1991, which added 7 percentage points to M2 growth.

8. It must be noted, however, that the local government budget position has benefited from increased State transfer payments to municipalities.

9. This reflects mainly two factors: the damping effect of lower interest rates on the surplus of the state pension fund (included in the consolidated central government but not the State budget), and a fall in the revenue contribution from taxes accrued but not paid. For a description of the relation between different budget concepts, see the OECD *Economic Survey of Norway* 1992/93, Annex I.

10. The "Long-Term Programme 1994-97" includes an *ex-post* evaluation of some of the projections contained in the previous programme, covering the period 1990 to 1993. This shows that total real transfers, including unemployment benefits, rose by an average annual rate of 4.5 per cent while Mainland output expanded by less than 1 per cent per year. This compares with projected real transfer growth of 1.5 per cent per year, below the expected 2.3 per cent annual growth rate for the Mainland economy. The overshooting was the result both of the incomplete implementation of suggested cuts and the introduction of new programmes or upgrading of existing ones, such as higher child support.

11. The only exception being the period 1986-89 when military spending was overestimated by a large margin.

12. This Commission, whose members represented a broad group of political parties, labour market organisations etc., published a report ("A National Strategy for Increased Employment") in August 1992.

13. A discussion of various oil income concepts is contained in Annex I of the 1991/92 OECD *Economic Survey* of Norway. Particularly in light of the low oil price in early 1994, the assessment of the permanent income level appears somewhat optimistic: a considerable rebound of oil prices is implied both in 1994 and 1998. In addition, the very high real interest rate of 7 per cent underlying the calculation also boosts the permanent income as discussed in the Survey referred to above. A lower rate of 5 per cent would reduce the permanent income from NKr 45 billion to 40.

14. "Generational Accounting in Norway: Is Norway Overconsuming its Oil Wealth?", Alan J. Auerbach *et al.*, July 1993.

15. "Statens naerings- og distriktsutviklingsfond" (SND), *i.e.* the State industrial and regional development fund.

16. NSB (railways), Postverket (postal service) and Televerket (telecommunications) are typical examples.

17. Including pay-roll taxes. The new legislation amounts to an increase in the pay-roll tax for wage earners with an annual wage income, inclusive of fringe benefits, in excess of NKr 584 000.

18. Pension funds are not subject to the wealth tax.

19. Sum of the standard capital income tax rate of 28 per cent and the capital income equivalent to the wealth tax, calculated on the basis of the current yield of 5.5 per cent on five-year government bonds.

20. "Mot bedre-Vitende", NOU 1991: 28.

21. "Agriculture as a Provider of Public Goods", Rolf Brunstad *et al.*, 1993.

22. "The Challenge of Enlargement. Commission Opinion on Norway's Application for Membership", EC Commission, 1993.

23. In the current membership negotiations, both Norway and Finland are confronted with this problem.

24. "Mot bedre-Vitende", NOU 1991: 28.

25. *Ibid.*

26. One such experiment, which started in 1993, is mentioned in the 1994 Budget: nine hospitals will have part of their expenses reimbursed on the basis of their output (*i.e.* the number of operations, etc.).

27. A similar assessment is made in a recent study entitled "Issues in Norwegian Banking" by Davis International Banking Consultants, which was commissioned by the Norwegian Ministry of Finance.

28. As envisaged in the Revised National Budget 1993, this process of partial privatisation started with "Christiania Bank og Kreditkasse" (CBK), with a new share issue which took place in late 1993. Over the period 1988 to 1992, CBK had received from the government almost NKr 10 billion, roughly one-third of the total funds used in rescue operations to the banking sector. As a result of better than expected developments in banking profitability, the National Budget for 1994 suggests that the process of privatisation could be accelerated.

29. OECD calculations based upon Table I in *Arbeidsmarkedstatistikk*, 1992.

30. See *OECD Employment Outlook*, July 1993, p.186.

31. Potential hours are defined as the total number of hours which would be worked if all working age individuals performed 37.5 hours per week 48 weeks per year.

32. Unemployed workers who leave the labour force because they think there is no work even though they would take such work were it offered.

33. Although unemployment rates among youths without high school education are very high, there are relatively few people who actually fall into this group.

34. This kind of aggregate wage behaviour is consistent with insider-outsider hysteresis models where institutional features impede market adjustment mechanisms so that the unemployed, and most especially the long-term unemployed, are excluded from the effective labour force and thus does not exert downward pressure on the wage level. See Blanchard and Summers (1986) and Lindbeck and Snower (1992) among others.

35. About as restrictive as in France, Germany and Sweden, but more restrictive than in Denmark and the United Kingdom.

36. See OECD *Employment Outlook* 1991 and 1993 which discuss the impact of unemployment insurance systems on aggregate unemployment. The balance of evidence in these surveys suggest that prolonged unemployment insurance benefits can lead to significant increases in structural unemployment.

37. By the end of 1989, the level of employment was the same as it would have been had employment continued to grow at about 1 per cent. The labour force, however, remained at artificially high levels.

38. Assuming 20 per cent unemployment and a 66 per cent replacement rate income under the benefit system would be equal to $80\% + (66\% \times 20\%) = 80 + 13.2 = 93\%$ of one's full-time income. Under the old regime the maximum duration was pro-rated so that the maximum benefits received by a full-time unemployed was the same as a partially unemployed person – hence the maximum duration of 80×5.

39. See OECD *Employment Outlook* 1991, pp. 206-207 and Pedersen and Westergaard, 1993, pp. 28-82 for more detailed discussion.

40. A discussion of the mechanisms whereby ALMP impact on labour market performance is contained in the OECD *Employment Outlook* (1993).

41. Similar results have been recorded in a number of other countries, including Denmark (Jensen *et al.*) and Sweden (Edin, 1988; Björklund, 1989, 1990; and Accum, 1991).

42. Preliminary research indicates that two-thirds of this increase is due to economic factors including rising unemployment, increased replacement ratios and higher female participation.

43. The OECD *Employment Outlook* 1993 contains a discussion of JPL's effects on the incentive to hire.

Bibliography

Accum, S. (1991), ''Youth Unemployment, Labour Market Programmes and Subsequent Earnings'', *Scandinavian Journal of Economics*, Vol. 93.

Auerbach, Alan J. (1993), ''Generational accounting in Norway: Is Norway overconsuming its oil wealth?'', Norwegian Research Council for applied Social Science.

Björklund, A. (1989), ''Klassiska experiment inom arbetsmarknadspolitiken'', *Rapport No. 37, 1989*, Industriens Utredningsinstitutt, Stockholm.

Björklund, A. (1990), ''Evaluations of Swedish Labour Market Policy'', *Finnish Economic Paper* Vol. 3.

Björklund, A. (1991), *Labour Market Policy and Unemployment Insurance*, Clarendon, Oxford.

Blanchard, O. and L. Summers (1986), ''Hysteresis and the European Unemployment Problem'', NBER Macroeconomic Annual, MIT press, Cambridge.

Brunstad *et al.* (1993), ''Agriculture as a Provider of Public Goods'', Norwegian Research Centre in Organisation and Management.

Commission of EC (1993), ''The Challenge of Enlargement. Commission Opinion on Norway's Application for Membership''.

Davis (1993), ''Issues in Norwegian Banking'', study commissioned by the Ministry of Finance, published Nov. 1993.

Edin, P.A. (1982), ''Individual Consequences of Plant Closures'', Department of Economics, Uppsala University.

Edin, P.A., B. Holmlund, and T. Ostros (1993), *Wage Behaviour and Labour Market Programmes in Sweden: Evidence from Micro Data*, Working Paper, Department of Economics, Uppsala University.

Jensen *et al.* (1991), ''Arbejdsmarkedsuddannelserne. Evaluering av effekten på arbejdsløshed og løn'', *Working Paper 1991:3*, Center for arbejdsmarkedsøkonomi, Handelshøjskolen i Århus og Universitetet i Århus.

Lindbeck A. and D. Snower (1988), *The Insider-Outsider Theory of Employment and Unemployment*, MIT Press, Cambridge, Massachusetts.

Long-Term Programme 1994-1997 (1993), Ministry of Finance.

Norges Offentlige Utredninger (1991:28), ''Mot bedre vitende?''.

Norges Offentlige Utredninger (1992:26), *En nasjonal strategi for økt sysselsetting i 1990 årene* (The Employment Commission). Abridged English version also available.

OECD (1991), *Employment Outlook*.

OECD (1992), *Employment Outlook*.

OECD (1993), *Employment Outlook*.

Pedersen, P.J. and N. Westergaard-Nielsen (1993), "Unemployment: A Review of the Evidence from Panel Data", OECD Economic Studies No. 20.

Raaum, O. and H. Torp (1993), "Evaluations of Labour Market Training Programmes: Some Experiences with an Experimental Design", Norwegian Ministry of Labour.

Annex

Calendar of main economic events

1992

January

The reformed tax code becomes effective.

April

The European Economic area agreement between the EFTA countries and the EC is signed.

Agreement between the largest trade union (LO) and the employers' Federation (NHO) for a wage increase of around NKr $\frac{1}{2}$ to $1\frac{1}{4}$ per hour. On average the settlement implies an annual increase in hourly wages of about 3 per cent.

The Commercial Bank Insurance Fund writes off about NKr 1.9 billion in preferential share capital in Fokus Bank in order to cover the bank's losses in 1991.

May

The Revised 1992 Budget is presented to Parliament:
  - The state budget deficit is expected to reach NKr $39\frac{1}{2}$ billion in 1992, exceeding the initial projections by close to NKr 10 billion. The increased expected deficit is mainly the result of a lower oil price assumption.
  - Excluding oil and gas revenue, the budget deficit is expected to be about NKr $71\frac{1}{2}$ billion, only slightly more than previously projected.

The Government and public employees agree at no increase in average hourly wages for 1992.

July

The Government authorises a merger between Forenede and Gjensidige, both medium-sized insurance companies. The new institution covers a substantial share of the market for pension and group life insurance.

August

Uni-Storebrand, the country's largest insurance company, is put under public administration. The company's assets, including the insurance business, are transferred to a new holding company.

Investa A/S, a larger finance company, declares bankruptcy.

The officially-appointed "Employment Commission" publishes its report "A National Strategy for Increased Employment". A description of the contents of this report is presented in the structural chapter of the present Survey.

September

The central bank extends its liquidity guarantee to include finance companies.

The "overnight" lending rate from the central bank to banks is increased by 1 percentage point to 11 per cent to defend the krone, following heavy speculation against the Finnish and Swedish currencies.

October

The 1993 Budget proposal is presented to Parliament:
- Based on an oil price assumption of NKr 127 per barrel, the state budget deficit for 1993 is projected to reach NKr 49.2 billion; excluding petroleum income the deficit should reach NKr 75.4 billion. Central government outlays are estimated to increase in line with mainland GDP.
- Reflecting the proposals of the Employment Commission, "active" labour market measures are strengthened. In order to limit the public sector deficit, this should be compensated by a reduction in transfers to households as a result of tighter conditions for disability pensions and sickness benefits.

November

The central bank cuts its "overnight" lending rate twice by $\frac{1}{2}$ percentage point to 10 per cent. But, following Sweden's decision to abandon the ecu link of the krona, the "overnight" lending rate to banks is increased again to 25 per cent to contain downward pressure on the Norwegian currency.

Den norske Bank, Christiania Bank and Fokus Bank – the three state-controlled commercial banks – received additional capital injections of NKr 4 billion and guarantees totalling NKr 800 million. In return, the banks agreed on a package of cost reductions of about 15 per cent. The state's ownership share of Den norske Bank is increased from 55 per cent to 70 per cent.

The Government applies for EC membership.

December

The central bank cuts the "overnight" lending rate to 17 per cent, as the pressure on the Norwegian krone weakens.

The 1993 Final Budget proposal is presented to Parliament:

– Several measures are introduced to revitalise the economy, including a 2.4 per cent reduction of payroll taxes, a cut in the electricity tax for energy intensive producers and increased regional subsidies. These measure are to be partly financed by a 2 per cent increase in the value-added tax.
– Given these new measures and revised income estimates, a budget deficit of NKr 51.4 billion is projected, NKr 2.3 billion higher than in the initial budget proposal. Excluding petroleum income the projected deficit is about NKr 76½ billion.

The Government decides to let the Norwegian krone float after heavy currency outflows. At the same time, the central bank cuts its "overnight" lending rate to 11 per cent.

1993

January

The central bank cuts its "overnight" lending rate twice by $\frac{1}{2}$ percentage point to 10 per cent.

February

The central bank progressively lowers its "overnight" lending rate to 9.25 per cent.

A Government Committee on VAT-reforms favour a continuation of the present uni-rate system.

March

The central bank cuts its "overnight" lending rate twice by ¼ percentage point, bringing it down to 8.75 per cent.

The Government Committee, appointed to suggest concrete cuts in transfers totalling NKr 5 billion, is not able to agree on a common proposal for reductions.

Following a writing down of the banks ordinary share capital, Den norske Bank receives a further NKr 1.5 billion from the Government Bank Insurance Fund.

April

The central bank lowers the overnight lending rate in four steps to 7.75 per cent.

Norway's negotiations on EC membership start.

A wage agreement is reached between LO and NHO, as the Government commits to provide to private pension schemes NKr 50 million for the lowering of the minimum retirement age. The agreement entails an increase in hourly wages of NKr 1 for workers not concerned by local negotiations and NKr ½ are for workers who may benefit from additional increases through local negotiations. Excluding the effect of local settlements, this amounts to a general wage increase of 1½ to 2 per cent.

May

The revised 1993 Budget is presented to Parliament. The state budget deficit is expected to reach NKr 54 billion in 1993, roughly NKr 5 billion above the level of the draft budget approved in December 1993, reflecting mainly lower revenues from both Mainland and oil activities.

The central bank cuts the "overnight" lending rate by ¼ percentage point to 7.50.

June

The central bank lowers the "overnight" lending rate in three steps to 7.25 per cent.

The Parliament adopts tax reliefs for persons located in the northern regions of Finnmark and Nor-Troms, amounting – for an average income person – to NKr 7 000 to 8 000 per year.

July

Seven leading gas producers sign a contract with German companies, implying an expansion of gas deliveries of 3.5 billion cubic meters per year, and a 10 to 15 per cent price rise.

September

After the general election to Parliament (Storting), the labour party remains in Government with strengthened parliamentary representation. The distribution of seats is the following (results from the previous election in 1989 are in brackets): Labour party 67 seats (63), Centre Party 32 seats (11), Conservatives 28 seats (32), Christian Peoples Party 13 seats (14), Socialist Left Party 13 seats (17), Progressive Party 10 seats (22), Liberals 1 seat (0) and Red Electorial Alliance 1 seat (0).

October

The newly formed Government presents the draft National Budget for 1994. Based upon an oil price of NKr 120 per barrel, the state budget deficit for 1994 is projected at NKr 46.4 billion; excluding oil-related revenues and expenditures the deficit is expected to reach NKr 72.5 billion.

The central bank reduces the ''overnight'' lending rate by $1/2$ percentage point to 7 per cent.

A coalition of the Government and the Christian Peoples Party agree on a formula for implementing an increase in the wealth tax, in line with the draft budget proposal.

November

The central bank cuts the ''overnight'' lending rate by $1/4$ percentage point to 6.75 per cent.

In the context of EC negotiations, the Norwegian Government presents a position paper on fishing, with the central tenet that fishing levels north of 62 latitude shall be decided by the Norwegian authorities.

December

The central bank raises the "overnight" lending rate by ¼ percentage point to 7 per cent.

The national budget for 1994 is adopted. Still based upon an oil price of NKr 120 per barrel, the state budget deficit is expected to be NKr 42.6 billion; exluding oil revenues and expenditures, the deficit is projected at NKr 70.3 billion.

STATISTICAL ANNEX

Selected background statistics

	Average 1983-92	1983	1984	1985	1986	1987	1988	1989	1990	1991	1992
A. Percentage changes											
Private consumption[1]	1.7	1.5	2.7	9.9	5.6	-1.0	-2.8	-2.8	2.8	0	1.8
Government consumption[1]	2.9	4.7	2.4	3.3	2.2	4.0	0.5	2.6	2.1	2.6	4.6
Gross fixed capital formation[1]	-0.8	5.8	10.9	-13.9	23.9	-2.1	1.6	-3.9	-26.8	1.7	3.5
Residential[1]	-7.1	0.8	-1.4	4.2	9.6	4.0	-3.8	-17.0	-17.1	-27.3	-15.9
Oil sector[1]	10.3	112.6	49.8	-42.9	62.4	-18.5	-4.2	25.0	-62.7	88.4	31.4
Ships and pipelines[1]	-24.3	-82.5	-385.0	-255.9	67.9	-61.9	-448.9	48.3	-62.0	-45.0	-111.5
Other private business sector[1]	-5.0	-15.0	-3.0	2.8	19.0	-2.2	-5.8	-17.2	-8.9	-13.0	-1.8
Public[1]	4.5	5.2	2.4	-3.6	15.1	10.0	7.4	0.7	-7.1	14.4	2.4
Total domestic demand[1]	1.2	1.1	6.0	4.7	8.0	-1.3	-3.1	-2.9	-0.9	-0.6	1.4
Exports of goods and services[1]	6.2	7.6	8.2	6.9	1.6	1.2	5.5	10.7	8.1	6.1	6.1
Imports of goods and services[1]	2.2	0	9.5	5.9	9.9	-7.3	-1.7	0.9	2.2	1.7	2.2
GDP[1]	2.8	4.6	5.7	5.3	4.2	2.1	-0.5	0.6	1.7	1.6	3.3
Mainland GDP[1]	1.5	2.7	3.8	5.9	3.4	1.2	-1.7	-2.2	1.1	-0.6	2.0
GDP price deflator	3.9	6.1	6.4	5.0	-1.4	7.2	4.4	5.9	4.5	2.4	-1.1
Industrial production	1.0	-1.6	2.8	8.1	1.1	1.0	-1.2	0.2	0.1	-1.6	1.4
Manufacturing	71.8	-0.8	3.6	4.8	1.0	1.1	-1.4	0.2	0	-1.5	2.2
Employment	0.3	0.1	1.3	2.3	3.5	1.9	-0.6	-3.0	-0.9	-1.0	-0.3
Compensation of employees (current prices)	7.2	8.1	9.1	10.8	13.2	12.9	5.9	1.3	4.1	4.2	3.5
Productivity (real GDP/employment)	2.5	4.5	4.4	2.9	0.6	0.2	0.1	3.7	2.6	2.6	3.6
Unit labour costs (compensation/real GDP)	4.3	3.3	3.2	5.2	8.7	10.6	6.4	0.7	2.4	2.6	0.2
B. Percentage ratios											
Gross fixed capital formation as percent of GDP at constant prices	22.9	25.7	26.9	22.0	26.2	25.1	25.6	24.5	17.6	17.6	17.7
Stockbuilding as per cent of GDP at constant prices	-0.2	-1.4	-0.4	2.2	1.1	0.1	-1.8	-2.6	1.4	0.2	-0.9
Foreign balance as per cent of GDP at constant prices	12.9	8.0	7.7	8.2	4.9	8.2	11.4	16.1	19.3	21.8	23.8
Compensation of employees as per cent of GDP at current prices	51.6	49.2	47.8	47.9	52.8	54.5	55.5	52.8	51.7	51.8	52.5
Direct taxes as per cent of household income	16.2	15.1	15.2	15.1	15.2	16.1	17.5	17.7	17.3	17.0	15.9
Household saving as per cent of disposable income	0.1	3.8	4.7	-2.5	-6.1	-6.2	-2.4	0.9	0.9	2.6	4.9
Unemployment rate	3.8	3.4	3.2	2.6	2.0	2.1	3.2	4.9	5.2	5.5	5.9
C. Other indicator											
Current balance (billion dollars)	0.8	2.0	2.9	3.1	-4.5	-4.1	-3.9	0.2	3.9	5.1	2.9
Excluding shipping and oil platforms	1.3	0.7	2.2	-3.6	-11.9	-8.9	5.0	19.6	10.6	2.9	-3.8

1. At constant prices.
Source: Central Bureau of Statistics; OECD estimates.

Table A. Supply and use of resources

Kr million, current prices

	1983	1984	1985	1986	1987	1988	1989	1990	1991	1992
Private consumption	192 958	210 892	245 369	278 952	298 030	307 560	311 946	336 065	349 689	364 999
Government consumption	78 213	84 100	92 654	101 580	116 045	122 238	130 998	139 116	147 478	157 368
Gross fixed investment	103 449	117 606	110 014	145 933	157 046	170 635	169 417	124 138	127 042	134 297
Stockbuilding	-4 246	-1 371	10 976	5 517	1 982	-12 245	-17 848	11 567	2 444	-5 921
Total domestic demand	370 374	411 227	459 013	531 982	573 103	588 188	594 513	610 886	626 652	650 743
Exports	183 859	214 058	235 767	194 854	200 257	213 638	261 816	292 776	307 543	303 028
Imports	152 031	172 859	194 605	213 178	211 451	218 040	234 515	242 837	247 090	251 723
GDP at market prices	402 202	452 427	500 176	513 659	561 909	583 786	621 814	660 825	687 106	702 048
Indirect taxes	69 733	78 200	91 037	99 922	107 493	106 984	106 562	111 089	115 617	121 707
Subsidies	24 439	25 709	26 936	29 569	31 515	33 769	36 599	39 992	42 858	44 981
GDP at factor costs	356 908	399 936	436 075	443 306	485 931	510 571	551 851	589 728	614 347	625 322
Depreciation and other operating provisions	59 619	62 427	66 488	72 502	83 730	91 703	97 110	99 098	102 970	104 744
Net domestic product at factor costs	297 289	337 509	369 587	370 804	402 201	418 868	454 741	490 630	511 377	520 578

Source: Norwegian National Accounts.

Table B. Gross domestic product by origin

Kr million, current prices

	1983	1984	1985	1986	1987	1988	1989	1990	1991	1992
Agriculture, forestry and fishing	13 135	15 042	15 150	16 021	17 695	17 689	17 568	20 330	20 052	..
Crude petroleum and natural gas production	66 855	83 386	89 706	50 966	51 759	44 383	69 755	86 912	89 670	..
Pipeline transport	2 506	2 483	2 987	5 663	5 987	5 966	7 136	7 962	9 994	..
Mining and quarrying	1 376	1 391	1 303	1 564	1 639	1 568	1 865	1 733	1 702	..
Manufacturing	56 724	64 524	70 127	75 651	84 590	89 506	91 265	90 368	92 591	..
Electricity supply	13 898	16 127	17 797	19 077	20 892	22 912	24 326	25 908	26 386	..
Construction	19 975	20 591	23 221	27 831	34 334	36 349	30 651	27 625	24 705	..
Wholesale and retail trade	40 328	43 668	47 298	54 694	58 893	61 197	61 426	64 934	66 663	..
Hotels and restaurants	5 147	5 776	6 598	7 871	9 225	9 033	8 558	8 284	8 652	..
Ocean transport and drilling	13 499	14 870	13 753	11 617	8 547	11 242	16 322	18 146	23 250	..
Other transports and communications	21 721	23 486	25 084	28 971	32 188	36 150	38 109	40 254	40 693	..
Financing and insurance	15 931	15 105	16 625	22 792	27 876	27 766	28 908	28 029	27 898	..
Business services	14 701	17 557	21 652	25 054	28 332	30 809	30 768	30 933	32 321	..
Dwelling services	15 001	16 656	18 105	19 711	21 796	25 367	28 940	32 287	33 811	..
Other private services	18 114	19 194	21 889	25 322	27 936	30 091	30 332	32 844	34 910	..
Producers of government services	56 841	61 808	67 965	75 370	85 629	91 930	97 841	104 125	111 910	..
Correction items	26 345	30 645	40 941	45 544	44 166	41 321	37 614	39 875	41 478	..
GDP at market prices	402 203	452 515	500 203	513 721	561 482	583 279	621 385	660 550	686 685	.

Source: Norwegian National Accounts.

Table C. **Gross domestic product by origin**

Volume, 1985 = 100

	1983	1984	1985	1986	1987	1988	1989	1990	1991	1992
Agriculture, forestry and fishing	101.4	109.9	100.0	94.1	98.5	99.6	102.5	114.2	115.3	113.3
Crude petroleum and natural gas production	83.3	96.4	100.0	106.4	120.5	135.2	171.3	176.4	201.3	226.6
Pipeline transport	81.7	87.4	100.0	169.2	190.6	185.5	220.3	217.6	239.2	266.5
Mining and quarrying	109.5	107.6	100.0	120.0	120.2	105.4	117.1	114.5	109.3	110.6
Manufacturing	91.2	96.5	100.0	100.0	101.9	97.0	95.4	96.1	94.0	95.7
Electricity, gas and water supply	99.5	103.0	100.0	92.7	98.7	105.1	115.7	116.2	104.8	111.1
Construction	94.5	94.8	100.0	109.8	113.8	112.7	103.7	99.5	94.0	93.1
Wholesale and retail trade	87.6	92.1	100.0	105.9	103.8	98.2	96.2	96.7	95.6	97.3
Hotels and restaurants	91.4	92.1	100.0	107.5	111.3	101.9	90.3	83.9	85.6	86.1
Ocean transport and drilling	95.7	102.4	100.0	97.4	77.0	73.9	88.1	102.4	106.3	102.5
Other transports and communications	92.1	95.4	100.0	109.0	112.7	120.5	120.6	127.9	133.7	131.5
Financing and insurance	93.6	93.5	100.0	104.7	111.7	115.1	106.6	102.4	95.9	93.9
Business services	80.0	87.4	100.0	104.3	108.7	108.2	103.0	96.1	95.0	96.9
Dwelling services	94.5	97.0	100.0	103.2	108.4	114.9	121.3	124.8	123.3	123.8
Other private services	94.1	93.4	100.0	107.3	107.7	108.7	104.9	107.7	108.7	112.0
Producers of government services	94.3	96.9	100.0	101.7	104.6	106.9	108.7	111.5	115.2	119.3
Correction items	..	..	100.0	105.8	93.7	76.7	64.6	66.9	67.1	71.0
GDP at market prices	89.8	95.0	100.0	104.2	106.3	105.7	106.4	108.1	109.8	113.5

Source: Norwegian National Accounts.

Table D. **General government income and expenditure**

Kr million

	1983	1984	1985	1986	1987	1988	1989	1990	1991	1992
Current receipts	208 208	239 826	275 435	281 097	309 816	321 356	341 444	371 880	379 324	384 489
Indirect taxes	69 733	78 200	91 037	99 922	107 493	106 984	106 562	111 089	115 617	121 707
Social security contributions	47 149	50 511	57 304	67 460	79 718	79 632	76 604	80 239	83 698	87 916
Direct taxes	76 721	87 637	100 600	79 309	87 951	96 505	107 395	118 449	120 050	118 519
Capital income	14 089	19 928	23 053	30 855	33 463	32 942	42 673	51 099	53 060	50 601
Other current receipts	516	3 550	3 441	3 551	1 191	5 293	8 210	11 004	6 899	5 746
Current expenditure	182 128	196 614	215 012	239 946	268 976	290 330	316 702	341 280	363 673	386 935
Expenditure on goods and services	78 213	84 100	92 654	101 580	116 045	122 238	130 998	139 116	147 478	157 368
Subsidies	24 439	25 709	26 936	29 569	31 515	33 769	36 599	39 992	42 858	44 823
Interest paid	13 414	15 018	17 393	22 325	24 061	22 670	24 705	25 805	24 836	25 996
Current transfers	3 850	3 870	4 210	4 947	5 283	6 295	6 249	7 385	7 630	8 077
Net saving	26 080	43 212	60 423	41 151	40 840	31 026	24 742	30 600	15 651	-2 446
Consumption of fixed capital	3 187	3 339	3 742	4 259	4 845	5 355	5 678	5 933	6 220	6 584
Gross saving	29 267	46 551	64 165	45 410	45 685	36 381	30 420	36 533	21 871	4 138
Gross fixed capital formation	12 410	12 858	13 288	16 458	20 087	22 650	23 020	21 423	24 307	24 958
Net lending	16 945	33 906	51 189	29 932	26 440	15 269	8 926	16 476	-1 536	-19 270
Memorandum item:										
Revenue from oil sector	36 076	44 260	50 598	18 268	15 402	9 940	24 573	40 684	42 077	39 892

Sources: Norwegian National Accounts; OECD, *National Accounts.*

Table E. Labour market
Thousand persons

	1983	1984	1985	1986	1987	1988	1989	1990	1991	1992
Civilian employment	1 910	1 939	1 984	2 053	2 090	2 079	2 014	1 992	1 973	1 970
Agriculture, forestry and fishing	148	143	147	151	139	134	132	129	116	110
Oil production and mining	18	21	22	22	24	24	23	22	21	25
Manufacturing	338	345	348	358	352	337	318	310	294	295
Electricity, gas and water	20	21	19	21	23	21	22	23	21	20
Construction	147	148	151	155	166	166	147	139	130	122
Wholesale and retail trade	336	330	346	364	375	376	369	358	354	353
Transports and communications	172	176	175	179	178	175	167	162	162	157
Banking, insurance, real estate	114	117	128	142	155	166	154	150	153	153
Community, social and personal services	614	635	644	658	673	674	675	696	716	729
Registered unemployment	63.5	66.6	51.4	36.2	32.4	49.3	82.9	92.7	100.7	114.4
Unfilled vacancies	3.3	4.3	5.8	10.5	12.4	8.7	6.9	6.6	6.5	6.4
Unemployment rate (per cent of labour force)	3.4	3.1	2.6	2.0	2.1	3.2	4.9	5.2	5.5	5.9

Sources: OECD, *Labour Force Statistics, Main Economic Indicators.*

Table F. **Balance of payments**

Million US dollars

	1983	1984	1985	1986	1987	1988	1989	1990	1991	1992
Current account										
Merchandise exports	18 069	19 099	19 937	18 158	21 179	23 053	27 174	34 072	34 095	35 165
Crude petroleum and natural gas	8 268	8 620	11 260	7 173	8 603	7 434	11 117	14 988	16 190	14 031
Ships and oil platforms	1 033	698	1 505	1 550	1 626	872	975	1 780	2 357	1 899
Other	8 769	9 781	7 172	9 435	10 950	14 747	15 082	17 304	15 547	19 235
Merchandise imports	13 698	13 934	15 199	20 250	21 899	23 239	23 392	26 475	25 439	25 866
Ships and oil platforms	1 001	641	693	625	978	2 310	3 919	3 051	2 334	1 004
Other	12 697	13 293	14 506	19 625	20 921	20 929	19 473	23 424	23 105	24 862
Trade balance	4 371	5 165	4 738	-2 092	-720	-186	3 782	7 598	8 656	9 299
Services, net	-1 781	-1 723	-1 078	-1 625	-2 360	-2 552	-2 416	-2 326	-2 037	-4 626
Travel	-1 025	-937	-1 067	-1 556	-1 853	-2 056	-1 642	-2 097	-1 770	-2 057
Investment income	-1 719	-1 540	-1 034	-1 129	-1 242	-1 955	-2 515	-2 676	-2 603	-3 469
Other services	963	754	1 023	1 060	735	1 459	1 741	2 447	2 336	900
Transfers, net	-583	-510	-555	-808	-979	-1 133	-1 128	-1 417	-1 513	-1 811
Private	-55	-35	-65	-140	-195	-167	-223	-236	-337	-491
Official	-528	-475	-490	-668	-784	-966	-905	-1 181	-1 176	-1 320
Current balance	2 007	2 931	3 105	-4 523	-4 058	-3 872	239	3 855	5 106	2 861
Capital account										
Long-term capital, net	-1 506	141	-1 030	2 817	19	4 599	3 027	-1 323	-3 018	3 701
Private, direct	-24	-822	-1 640	-582	-706	-683	159	-474	-2 142	433
Private, portfolio	-884	889	1 744	4 286	2 346	4 185	3 060	514	-3 087	2 062
Private, other	-265	186	-1 045	-734	-1 558	1 230	-188	-1 568	2 010	1 130
Public[1]	-335	-112	-89	-152	-63	-132	-2	207	203	75
Short-term capital, net	-1 008	418	2 583	113	5 500	108	-1 034	641	-4 775	-4 658
Private non monetary	-1 205	57	182	1 285	317	155	-658	360	824	2 214
Private monetary institutions	197	361	2 401	-1 172	5 183	-47	-376	281	-5 599	-6 872
Miscellaneous official accounts	8	-43	-1	25	-25	65	-58	-37	40	750
Allocation of SDRs	0	0	0	0	0	0	0	0	0	0
Errors and omissions	386	-384	-1 199	-1 650	-1 257	-1 063	-1 355	-2 804	-146	-3 254
Change in reserves	-87	3 055	3 446	-3 168	-84	-225	902	355	-2 766	-625

1. Excludes special transactions.
Source: OECD Secretariat.

Table G. Foreign trade by area
Million US dollars

	1982	1983	1984	1985	1986	1987	1988	1989	1990	1991
Imports, total	15 481	13 494	13 885	15 554	20 298	22 578	23 211	23 668	27 200	25 523
OECD countries	13 470	11 979	12 268	13 935	18 521	20 220	19 275	18 222	22 385	21 528
EEC	7 051	6 291	6 549	7 643	10 163	11 196	10 638	10 085	12 335	12 211
of which: Germany	2 403	1 987	2 007	2 500	3 436	3 495	3 145	2 972	3 768	3 608
Belgium-Luxembourg	360	346	384	433	596	650	585	618	634	612
France	522	486	636	650	824	832	767	770	1 009	975
Netherlands	529	484	478	550	775	868	906	781	1 068	1 341
United Kingdom	1 668	1 407	1 426	1 553	1 783	2 020	1 724	1 681	2 325	2 128
USA	1 419	1 233	1 243	1 118	1 393	1 452	1 527	1 724	2 388	1 986
Sweden	2 647	2 535	2 383	2 776	3 644	4 265	4 071	3 586	4 234	3 927
Finland	701	470	673	632	811	981	808	711	843	804
Non OECD countries	1 840	1 515	1 616	1 619	1 768	2 347	3 792	5 290	4 687	3 880
COMECON	571	485	502	434	366	445	528	593	685	544
OPEC	142	100	102	128	82	65	112	117	144	127
Others	1 127	930	1 013	1 058	1 320	1 837	3 152	4 580	3 858	3 208
Exports, total	17 582	17 972	18 914	19 934	18 230	21 449	22 429	27 101	34 033	34 037
OECD countries	15 650	16 287	17 186	17 682	15 689	18 875	20 073	24 536	30 643	30 424
EEC	12 781	12 627	13 377	13 846	11 859	13 803	14 343	17 324	21 653	22 262
of which: Germany	3 518	3 410	3 120	3 104	3 485	3 193	2 699	2 934	3 680	3 703
Belgium-Luxembourg	188	183	170	193	215	288	557	672	723	821
France	389	494	642	1 048	627	1 086	1 596	2 380	2 606	2 537
Netherlands	1 113	1 283	1 379	1 214	1 086	1 562	1 497	1 753	2 636	2 668
United Kingdom	6 434	6 164	6 892	7 103	5 060	5 711	5 786	7 221	8 853	8 937
USA	484	768	964	1 021	988	1 222	1 334	1 775	2 168	1 609
Sweden	1 587	1 819	1 865	1 752	1 805	2 387	2 564	3 238	3 834	3 447
Finland	281	349	276	315	317	421	468	558	916	1 014
Non OECD countries	1 931	1 686	1 728	2 251	2 541	2 574	1 715	1 796	2 622	2 971
COMECON	214	220	164	175	174	223	270	287	382	406
OPEC	227	204	102	100	122	112	100	94	413	116
Others	1 491	1 262	1 462	1 977	2 246	2 240	1 345	1 415	1 826	2 449

Source: OECD, *Foreign Trade Statistics, Series C.*

Table H. **Prices and wages**

1985 = 100

	1983	1984	1985	1986	1987	1988	1989	1990	1991	1992
Consumer prices										
Total	89.0	94.6	100.0	107.2	116.5	124.3	130.0	135.4	140.0	143.3
Food	87.9	93.9	100.0	109.2	117.5	124.9	128.4	132.5	134.8	136.7
Rent, heating and light	87.7	94.4	100.0	105.0	112.8	122.1	129.5	137.8	144.0	147.4
Wholesale prices										
Total	89.4	95.1	100.0	102.6	108.7	114.5	120.8	125.2	128.4	128.5
Consumer goods	89.1	94.8	100.0	105.8	113.0	119.4	124.3	130.0	134.8	137.2
Investment goods	92.4	96.1	100.0	106.9	113.6	118.7	122.9	125.5	128.2	129.3
Petroleum products	95.1	98.8	100.0	69.6	73.3	65.6	76.1	90.2	90.4	82.4
Hourly earnings										
Males	85.8	93.1	100.0	110.2	127.9	135.2	141.9	149.6	158.2	163.2
Females	85.8	93.0	100.0	110.5	128.3	136.3	144.7	153.4	163.5	168.8

Source: OECD, *Main Economic Indicators*, Secretariat estimates.

Table I. **Money and credit**

Kr million

	1983	1984	1985	1986	1987	1988	1989	1990	1991	1992
Changes in money supply										
Central authorities[1]	20 089	19 285	10 566	-3 696	16 784	16 568	34 836	46 465	60 308	77 126
Commercial and saving banks[2]	13 735	32 259	63 677	50 651	83 298	11 290	1 303	1 076	12 520	-26 970
Unspecified and statistical errors	-1 982	-946	-940	14 695	-9 739	-6 200	-17 396	-17 498	-8 811	-10 086
Domestic liquidity supply	31 842	50 598	73 303	61 650	90 343	21 658	18 743	30 043	64 017	40 070
Foreign transactions	-12 049	-5 062	-31 572	-47 176	-40 252	300	11 794	-4 147	-15 101	-2 964
Change in broad money (M2)	19 793	45 536	41 729	14 474	50 091	21 958	30 537	25 896	48 916	37 106
Domestic lending by financial institutions										
Total[3]	339 797	392 711	470 984	571 850	692 160	765 431	823 750	843 200	823 585	811 089
Commercial banks	81 937	104 099	132 679	173 610	211 822	222 678	247 639	250 987	231 892	252 939
Saving banks	61 667	77 534	104 056	129 822	159 072	173 158	184 100	191 950	191 652	200 310
State banks	108 357	116 708	121 793	129 559	137 446	145 777	154 725	163 044	174 949	185 586
Insurance companies	25 899	30 192	36 971	46 809	55 597	59 414	59 313	60 975	69 780	79 336
Mortgage credit institutions	40 121	46 145	52 774	67 467	99 870	126 488	142 782	144 659	121 606	83 280
Private finance institutions	11 342	13 093	17 355	18 751	21 898	30 347	25 963	20 742	19 986	17 719
Postal saving banks	4 090	4 557	4 993	5 460	6 047	7 101	8 394	10 196	13 089	15 235

1. Government income surplus, loan transactions, Central and State banks. Excluding oil taxes.
2. Including tax-free allocations to funds and saving with tax productions.
3. Breakdown does not add up to total.
Sources: Bank of Norway, *Economic Bulletin*; Central Bureau of Statistics, *Monthly Bulletin of Statistics*.

Table J. **Production and employment structures**

	Per cent share of GDP at factor cost (current prices)				Per cent share of total employment			
	1962	1970	1980	1991	1962	1970	1980	1991
Agriculture, forestry and fishing	7.9	5.6	3.8	2.9	19.0	12.9	8.4	6.1
Mining, crude petroleum and natural gas	0.8	0.7	14.8	13.3	0.6	0.6	0.8	1.1
Manufacturing	21.1	21.6	16.0	13.5	23.4	23.8	19.8	14.3
Of which: Food, forestry and tobacco	3.9	3.3	1.7	3.0	3.7	3.6	3.1	2.5
Textiles, clothing, leather	2.3	1.5	0.7	0.3	3.2	2.4	1.2	0.5
Wood and wood products	1.6	1.8	1.4	0.8	2.1	2.2	1.9	1.2
Paper and paper products	2.6	2.8	2.0	2.1	3.4	3.5	2.8	2.4
Chemicals and products of petroleum, coal, rubber, etc.	2.1	2.3	1.9	1.6	3.0	3.0	2.5	1.9
Fabricated metal products, machinery and equipment	5.7	6.4	5.6	4.3	6.4	7.4	6.8	4.9
Electricity, gas and water	2.8	2.7	2.9	4.0	0.9	0.9	0.9	1.0
Construction	8.0	7.0	5.9	3.9	8.1	8.2	7.9	6.9
Services	59.4	62.4	56.5	62.4	48.2	53.7	62.3	70.6
Of which: Wholesale and retail trade, restaurants, and hotels	20.1	12.4	11.7	11.0	14.4	15.5	16.6	16.5
Transport, storage and communication	14.7	14.7	9.4	10.4	11.2	10.2	9.1	8.9
Finance, insurance, real estate and business services	9.5	9.1	9.9	13.7	2.7	3.7	5.0	7.3
Producers of Government services	9.7	11.8	13.6	16.3	12.8	16.6	23.2	28.7

Source: OECD, *National Accounts.*

108

Table K. **Productivity and investment structure**

	Productivity growth (Sector GDP/sector employment)				Investment Per cent of total investment[1]			
	1963-69	1970-79	1980-91	1991	1962	1970	1980	1991
Agriculture, forestry and fishing	4.4	3.3	4.6	5.6	8.0	6.6	8.2	3.8
Mining, crude petroleum and natural gas	8.7	25.7	6.5	9.5	0.6	2.4	9.7	20.5
Manufacturing	4.6	1.7	2.3	1.4	17.1	15.3	12.8	10.3
Of which: Food, forestry and tobacco	3.8	0.2	−0.1	4.5	3.2	2.9	2.3	2.0
Textiles, clothing, leather	3.1	0.6	4.2	8.0	0.7	0.5	0.4	0.1
Wood and wood products	6.4	1.6	0.5	−0.1	0.5	1.2	0.8	0.6
Paper and paper products	5.2	−0.1	2.0	0.4	2.8	1.8	3.0	1.7
Chemicals and products of petroleum, coal, rubber, etc.	8.1	4.0	4.8	−8.1	3.3	2.0	1.4	2.0
Fabricated metal products, machinery and equipment	2.9	1.3	2.4	3.5	3.4	3.4	2.6	2.1
Electricity, gas and water	5.2	0.7	0.7	−8.3	10.4	8.1	9.9	5.1
Construction	2.8	2.5	0.2	3.3	1.3	2.0	2.2	1.8
Services	2.4	0.5	−1.3	−4.2	62.6	65.5	57.3	58.5
Of which: Wholesale and retail trade, restaurants and hotels	1.3	−0.6	−0.2	1.7	4.7	4.6	4.6	4.2
Transport, storage and communication	4.5	3.3	3.7	5.1	25.8	20.5	10.9	16.7
Finance, insurance, real estate and business services	−0.2	−1.6	−1.8	−0.9	19.2	21.8	23.9	16.6
Producers of Government services	2.0	0.5	0.8	0.3	12.1	16.9	16.2	19.1

1. At current prices.
Source: OECD, *National Accounts.*

Table L. **Labour-market indicators**

A. LABOUR MARKET PERFORMANCE

	Cyclical Trough: 1983	Cyclical Peak: 1986	1988	1992
Standardised unemployment rate	3.4	2.0	3.2	5.9
Unemployment rate: Total	3.4	2.0	3.1	5.9
Male	3.2	1.6	3.0	6.6
Women	3.8	2.4	3.3	5.1
Youth[1]	8.9	5.0	7.9	13.9
Share of long-term unemployment in total unemployment[2]	5.8	7.1	5.8	20.6

B. STRUCTURAL OR INSTITUTIONAL CHARACTERISTICS

	1975	1980	1985	1992
Participation rate[3]: Total	69.8	76.7	80.0	78.2
Male	85.5	88.7	89.7	84.2
Women	53.6	64.2	70.1	71.9
Employment/population (15-64 years)	69.1	74.0	75.5	73.2
Non-wage labour costs[4] (as a percentage of total compensation)	14.9	14.6	14.3	14.9
Unemployment insurance replacement ratio[5]	7.2	23.6	34.9	40.2

Average percentage changes (annual rates)	1970 / 1960	1980 / 1970	1990 / 1980	1992 / 1991
Labour force	0.7	2.2	1.3	0.2
Employment: Total	0.7	2.1	1.2	–0.3
Industries	1.2	0	–0.7	–1.1
Services	2.0	4.7	2.4	0.6

1. People between 16 and 24 years as a percentage of the labour force of the same age group.
2. Persons seeking a job for 12 months and over as a percentage of total unemployed.
3. Labour force as a percentage of relevant population group, aged between 15 and 64 years.
4. Employers'contributions to social security and pension funds.
5. Unemployment benefits per unemployed as a percentage of compensation per employee.
Sources: OECD, *Labour Force Statistics;* OECD Secretariat.

Table M. **Public sector**

General government income and expenditure structures

As a percentage of GDP

	1962	1970	1980	1991
Current receipts	35.5	43.5	53.2	55.2
Indirect taxes	14.1	18.2	17.2	16.8
Social security contributions	6.3	9.7	12.0	12.2
Direct taxes	13.4	13.3	21.5	17.5
Capital income	1.7	2.3	2.5	7.7
Other current receipts	0	0	0.1	1.0
Current expenditure	28.0	36.5	44.3	52.9
Expenditure on goods and services	14.0	16.9	18.8	21.5
Defence	3.4	3.5	2.8	3.2
Education	3.7	4.9	5.1	5.5
Health	1.5	2.4	4.1	4.9
Social security and welfare	0.8	0.9	1.6	2.3
Economic services	2.2	2.4	2.3	2.2
Other	2.5	2.8	2.9	3.4
Subsidies	4.2	5.2	7.0	6.2
Interest paid	1.5	1.8	3.4	3.6
Current transfers	8.4	12.6	15.1	21.6
Net saving	7.6	7.0	8.9	2.3
Consumption of fixed capital	0.6	0.7	0.8	0.9
Gross saving	8.1	7.7	9.7	3.2
Gross fixed capital formation	3.5	4.5	4.0	3.5
Net lending	4.6	3.2	5.7	−0.2
Memorandum item:				
Revenue from oil sector	0	0	8.2	4.1

Sources: Norwegian National Accounts; *OECD National Accounts.*

BASIC STATISTICS:
INTERNATIONAL COMPARISONS

	Units	Reference period[1]	Australia	Austria	Belgium	Canada
Population						
Total	Thousands	1990	17 085	7 718	9 967	26 620
Inhabitants per sq. km	Number	1990	2	92	327	3
Net average annual increase over previous 10 years . . .	%	1990	1.5	0.2	0.1	1
Employment						
Total civilian employment (TCE)[2]	Thousands	1990	7 850	3 412	3 726	12 572
Of which : Agriculture...................	% of TCE		5.6	7.9	2.7	4.2
Industry	% of TCE		25.4	36.8	28.3	24.6
Services	% of TCE		69	55.3	69	71.2
Gross domestic product (GDP)						
At current prices and current exchange rates	Bill US $	1990	294.1	157.4	192.4	570.1
Per capita	US $		17 215	20 391	19 303	21 418
At current prices using current PPP's[3]	Bill US $	1990	271.7	127.4	163	510.5
Per capita	US $		15 900	16 513	16 351	19 179
Average annual volume growth over previous 5 years .	%	1990	3.1	3.1	3.2	3
Gross fixed capital formation (GFCF)	% of GDP	1990	22.9	24.3	20.3	21.4
Of which: Machinery and equipment	% of GDP		9.7	10.1	10.4	7.2
Residential construction	% of GDP	1990	4.8	4.6	4.3	6.8
Average annual volume growth over previous 5 years .	%	1990	2.4	4.6	9.5	5.8
Gross saving ratio[4]	% of GDP	1990	19.7	26	21.8	17.4
General government						
Current expenditure on goods and services	% of GDP	1990	17.3	18	14.3	19.8
Current disbursements[5]	% of GDP	1990	34.9	44.9	53.1	44
Current receipts	% of GDP	1990	35.1	46.7	49.5	41.6
Net official development assistance	Mill US $	1990	0.34	0.25	0.45	0.44
Indicators of living standards						
Private consumption per capita using current PPP's[3]	US $	1990	9 441	9 154	10 119	11 323
Passenger cars per 1 000 inhabitants	Number	1989	570	416	416	613
Telephones per 1 000 inhabitants	Number	1989	550 (85)	540	500 (88)	780 (8
Television sets per 1 000 inhabitants	Number	1988	217	484 (89)	255	586
Doctors per 1 000 inhabitants	Number	1990	2.3	2.1	3.4	2.2
Infant mortality per 1 000 live births	Number	1990	8.1	7.8	7.9	7.2 (8
Wages and prices (average annual increase over previous 5 years)						
Wages (earnings or rates according to availability) . . .	%	1990	5.6	5	3	4.3
Consumer prices	%	1990	7.9	2.2	2.1	4.5
Foreign trade						
Exports of goods, fob*	Mill US $	1990	39 813	40 985	118 291[7]	127 334
As % of GDP	%		13.5	26	61.5	22.3
Average annual increase over previous 5 years . . .	%		11.9	19.1	17.1	7.8
Imports of goods, cif*	Mill US $	1990	38 907	48 914	120 330[7]	116 561
As % of GDP	%		13.2	31.1	62.5	20.4
Average annual increase over previous 5 years . . .	%		11	18.6	16.5	8.8
Total official reserves[6]	Mill SDR's	1990	11 432	6 591	8 541[7]	12 544
As ratio of average monthly imports of goods	ratio		3.5	1.6	0.9	1.3

* At current prices and exchange rates.
1. Unless otherwise stated.
2. According to the definitions used in OECD Labour Force Statistics.
3. PPP's = Purchasing Power Parities.
4. Gross saving = Gross national disposable income minus Private and Government consumption.
5. Current disbursements = Current expenditure on goods and services plus current transfers and payments of property income.
6. Gold included in reserves is valued at 35 SDR's per ounce. End of year.
7. Including Luxembourg.
8. Included in Belgium.

EMPLOYMENT OPPORTUNITIES

Economics Department, OECD

The Economics Department of the OECD offers challenging and rewarding opportunities to economists interested in applied policy analysis in an international environment. The Department's concerns extend across the entire field of economic policy analysis, both macro-economic and micro-economic. Its main task is to provide, for discussion by committees of senior officials from Member countries, documents and papers dealing with current policy concerns. Within this programme of work, three major responsibilities are:

- to prepare regular surveys of the economies of individual Member countries;
- to issue full twice-yearly reviews of the economic situation and prospects of the OECD countries in the context of world economic trends;
- to analyse specific policy issues in a medium-term context for theOECD as a whole, and to a lesser extent for the non-OECD countries.

The documents prepared for these purposes, together with much of the Department's other economic work, appear in published form in the *OECD Economic Outlook, OECD Economic Surveys, OECD Economic Studies* and the Department's *Working Papers* series.

The Department maintains a world econometric model, INTERLINK, which plays an important role in the preparation of the policy analyses and twice-yearly projections. The availability of extensive cross-country data bases and good computer resources facilitates comparative empirical analysis, much of which is incorporated into the model.

The Department is made up of about 75 professional economists from a variety of backgrounds and Member countries. Most projects are carried out by small teams and last from four to eighteen months. Within the Department, ideas and points of view are widely discussed; there is a lively professional interchange, and all professional staff have the opportunity to contribute actively to the programme of work.

Skills the Economics Department is looking for:

a) Solid competence in using the tools of both micro-economic and macro-economic theory to answer policy questions. Experience indicates that this normally requires the equivalent of a PH.D. in economics or substantial relevant professional experience to compensate for a lower degree.

b) Solid knowledge of economic statistics and quantitative methods; this includes how to identify data, estimate structural relationships, apply basic techniques of time series analysis, and test hypotheses. It is essential to be able to interpret results sensibly in an economic policy context.

c) A keen interest in and knowledge of policy issues, economic developments and their political/social contexts.

d) Interest and experience in analysing questions posed by policy-makers and presenting the results to them effectively and judiciously. Thus, work experience in government agencies or policy research institutions is an advantage.

e) The ability to write clearly, effectively, and to the point. The OECD is a bilingual organisation with French and English as the official languages. Candidates must have excellent knowledge of one of these languages, and some knowledge of the other. Knowledge of other languages might also be an advantage for certain posts.

f) For some posts, expertise in a particular area may be important, but a successful candidate is expected to be able to work on a broader range of topics relevant to the work of the Department. Thus, except in rare cases, the Department does not recruit narrow specialists.

g) The Department works on a tight time schedule and strict deadlines. Moreover, much of the work in the Department is carried out in small groups of economists. Thus, the ability to work with other economists from a variety of cultural and professional backgrounds, to supervise junior staff, and to produce work on time is important.

General Information

The salary for recruits depends on educational and professional background. Positions carry a basic salary from FF 262 512 or FF 323 916 for Administrators (economists) and from FF 375 708 for Principal Administrators (senior economists). This may be supplemented by expatriation and/or family allowances, depending on nationality, residence and family situation. Initial appointments are for a fixed term of two to three years.

Vacancies are open to candidates from OECD Member countries. The Organisation seeks to maintain an appropriate balance between female and male staff and among nationals from Member countries.

For further information on employment opportunities in the Economics Department, contact:

Administrative Unit
Economics Department
OECD
2, rue André-Pascal
75775 PARIS CEDEX 16
FRANCE

Applications citing "ECSUR", together with a detailed *curriculum vitae* in English or French, should be sent to the Head of Personnel at the above address.

MAIN SALES OUTLETS OF OECD PUBLICATIONS
PRINCIPAUX POINTS DE VENTE DES PUBLICATIONS DE L'OCDE

ARGENTINA – ARGENTINE
Carlos Hirsch S.R.L.
Galería Güemes, Florida 165, 4° Piso
1333 Buenos Aires   Tel. (1) 331.1787 y 331.2391
Telefax: (1) 331.1787

AUSTRALIA – AUSTRALIE
D.A. Information Services
648 Whitehorse Road, P.O.B 163
Mitcham, Victoria 3132   Tel. (03) 873.4411
Telefax: (03) 873.5679

AUSTRIA – AUTRICHE
Gerold & Co.
Graben 31
Wien I   Tel. (0222) 533.50.14

BELGIUM – BELGIQUE
Jean De Lannoy
Avenue du Roi 202
B-1060 Bruxelles   Tel. (02) 538.51.69/538.08.41
Telefax: (02) 538.08.41

CANADA
Renouf Publishing Company Ltd.
1294 Algoma Road
Ottawa, ON K1B 3W8   Tel. (613) 741.4333
Telefax: (613) 741.5439
Stores:
61 Sparks Street
Ottawa, ON K1P 5R1   Tel. (613) 238.8985
211 Yonge Street
Toronto, ON M5B 1M4   Tel. (416) 363.3171
Telefax: (416)363.59.63
Les Éditions La Liberté Inc.
3020 Chemin Sainte-Foy
Sainte-Foy, PQ G1X 3V6   Tel. (418) 658.3763
Telefax: (418) 658.3763

Federal Publications Inc.
165 University Avenue, Suite 701
Toronto, ON M5H 3B8   Tel. (416) 860.1611
Telefax: (416) 860.1608

Les Publications Fédérales
1185 Université
Montréal, QC H3B 3A7   Tel. (514) 954.1633
Telefax : (514) 954.1635

CHINA – CHINE
China National Publications Import
Export Corporation (CNPIEC)
16 Gongti E. Road, Chaoyang District
P.O. Box 88 or 50
Beijing 100704 PR   Tel. (01) 506.6688
Telefax: (01) 506.3101

DENMARK – DANEMARK
Munksgaard Book and Subscription Service
35, Nørre Søgade, P.O. Box 2148
DK-1016 København K   Tel. (33) 12.85.70
Telefax: (33) 12.93.87

FINLAND – FINLANDE
Akateeminen Kirjakauppa
Keskuskatu 1, P.O. Box 128
00100 Helsinki

Subscription Services/Agence d'abonnements :
P.O. Box 23
00371 Helsinki   Tel. (358 0) 12141
Telefax: (358 0) 121.4450

FRANCE
OECD/OCDE
Mail Orders/Commandes par correspondance:
2, rue André-Pascal
75775 Paris Cedex 16   Tel. (33-1) 45.24.82.00
Telefax: (33-1) 45.24.81.76   or (33-1) 45.24.85.00
Telex: 640048 OCDE

OECD Bookshop/Librairie de l'OCDE :
33, rue Octave-Feuillet
75016 Paris   Tel. (33-1) 45.24.81.67
(33-1) 45.24.81.81
Documentation Française
29, quai Voltaire
75007 Paris   Tel. 40.15.70.00
Gibert Jeune (Droit-Économie)
6, place Saint-Michel
75006 Paris   Tel. 43.25.91.19
Librairie du Commerce International
10, avenue d'Iéna
75016 Paris   Tel. 40.73.34.60
Librairie Dunod
Université Paris-Dauphine
Place du Maréchal de Lattre de Tassigny
75016 Paris   Tel. (1) 44.05.40.13
Librairie Lavoisier
11, rue Lavoisier
75008 Paris   Tel. 42.65.39.95
Librairie L.G.D.J. - Montchrestien
20, rue Soufflot
75005 Paris   Tel. 46.33.89.85
Librairie des Sciences Politiques
30, rue Saint-Guillaume
75007 Paris   Tel. 45.48.36.02
P.U.F.
49, boulevard Saint-Michel
75005 Paris   Tel. 43.25.83.40
Librairie de l'Université
12a, rue Nazareth
13100 Aix-en-Provence   Tel. (16) 42.26.18.08
Documentation Française
165, rue Garibaldi
69003 Lyon   Tel. (16) 78.63.32.23
Librairie Decitre
29, place Bellecour
69002 Lyon   Tel. (16) 72.40.54.54

GERMANY – ALLEMAGNE
OECD Publications and Information Centre
August-Bebel-Allee 6
D-53175 Bonn 2   Tel. (0228) 959.120
Telefax: (0228) 959.12.17

GREECE – GRÈCE
Librairie Kauffmann
Mavrokordatou 9
106 78 Athens   Tel. (01) 32.55.321
Telefax: (01) 36.33.967

HONG-KONG
Swindon Book Co. Ltd.
13–15 Lock Road
Kowloon, Hong Kong   Tel. 366.80.31
Telefax: 739.49.75

HUNGARY – HONGRIE
Euro Info Service
POB 1271
1464 Budapest   Tel. (1) 111.62.16
Telefax : (1) 111.60.61

ICELAND – ISLANDE
Mál Mog Menning
Laugavegi 18, Pósthólf 392
121 Reykjavik   Tel. 162.35.23

INDIA – INDE
Oxford Book and Stationery Co.
Scindia House
New Delhi 110001   Tel.(11) 331.5896/5308
Telefax: (11) 332.5993
17 Park Street
Calcutta 700016   Tel. 240832

INDONESIA – INDONÉSIE
Pdii-Lipi
P.O. Box 269/JKSMG/88
Jakarta 12790   Tel. 583467
Telex: 62 875

IRELAND – IRLANDE
TDC Publishers – Library Suppliers
12 North Frederick Street
Dublin 1   Tel. (01) 874.48.35
Telefax: (01) 874.84.16

ISRAEL
Electronic Publications only
Publications électroniques seulement
Sophist Systems Ltd.
71 Allenby Street
Tel-Aviv 65134   Tel. 3-29.00.21
Telefax: 3-29.92.39

ITALY – ITALIE
Libreria Commissionaria Sansoni
Via Duca di Calabria 1/1
50125 Firenze   Tel. (055) 64.54.15
Telefax: (055) 64.12.57
Via Bartolini 29
20155 Milano   Tel. (02) 36.50.83
Editrice e Libreria Herder
Piazza Montecitorio 120
00186 Roma   Tel. 679.46.28
Telefax: 678.47.51
Libreria Hoepli
Via Hoepli 5
20121 Milano   Tel. (02) 86.54.46
Telefax: (02) 805.28.86
Libreria Scientifica
Dott. Lucio de Biasio 'Aeiou'
Via Coronelli, 6
20146 Milano   Tel. (02) 48.95.45.52
Telefax: (02) 48.95.45.48

JAPAN – JAPON
OECD Publications and Information Centre
Landic Akasaka Building
2-3-4 Akasaka, Minato-ku
Tokyo 107   Tel. (81.3) 3586.2016
Telefax: (81.3) 3584.7929

KOREA – CORÉE
Kyobo Book Centre Co. Ltd.
P.O. Box 1658, Kwang Hwa Moon
Seoul   Tel. 730.78.91
Telefax: 735.00.30

MALAYSIA – MALAISIE
Co-operative Bookshop Ltd.
University of Malaya
P.O. Box 1127, Jalan Pantai Baru
59700 Kuala Lumpur
Malaysia   Tel. 756.5000/756.5425
Telefax: 757.3661

MEXICO – MEXIQUE
Revistas y Periodicos Internacionales S.A. de C.V.
Florencia 57 - 1004
Mexico, D.F. 06600   Tel. 207.81.00
Telefax : 208.39.79

NETHERLANDS – PAYS-BAS
SDU Uitgeverij Plantijnstraat
Externe Fondsen
Postbus 20014
2500 EA's-Gravenhage   Tel. (070) 37.89.880
Voor bestellingen: Telefax: (070) 34.75.778

NEW ZEALAND
NOUVELLE-ZÉLANDE
Legislation Services
P.O. Box 12418
Thorndon, Wellington   Tel. (04) 496.5652
                              Telefax: (04) 496.5698

NORWAY – NORVÈGE
Narvesen Info Center – NIC
Bertrand Narvesens vei 2
P.O. Box 6125 Etterstad
0602 Oslo 6   Tel. (022) 57.33.00
                              Telefax: (022) 68.19.01

PAKISTAN
Mirza Book Agency
65 Shahrah Quaid-E-Azam
Lahore 54000   Tel. (42) 353.601
                              Telefax: (42) 231.730

PHILIPPINE – PHILIPPINES
International Book Center
5th Floor, Filipinas Life Bldg.
Ayala Avenue
Metro Manila   Tel. 81.96.76
                              Telex 23312 RHP PH

PORTUGAL
Livraria Portugal
Rua do Carmo 70-74
Apart. 2681
1200 Lisboa   Tel.: (01) 347.49.82/5
                              Telefax: (01) 347.02.64

SINGAPORE – SINGAPOUR
Gower Asia Pacific Pte Ltd.
Golden Wheel Building
41, Kallang Pudding Road, No. 04-03
Singapore 1334   Tel. 741.5166
                              Telefax: 742.9356

SPAIN – ESPAGNE
Mundi-Prensa Libros S.A.
Castelló 37, Apartado 1223
Madrid 28001   Tel. (91) 431.33.99
                              Telefax: (91) 575.39.98

Libreria Internacional AEDOS
Consejo de Ciento 391
08009 – Barcelona   Tel. (93) 488.30.09
                              Telefax: (93) 487.76.59
Llibreria de la Generalitat
Palau Moja
Rambla dels Estudis, 118
08002 – Barcelona
           (Subscripcions) Tel. (93) 318.80.12
           (Publicacions) Tel. (93) 302.67.23
                              Telefax: (93) 412.18.54

SRI LANKA
Centre for Policy Research
c/o Colombo Agencies Ltd.
No. 300-304, Galle Road
Colombo 3   Tel. (1) 574240, 573551-2
                              Telefax: (1) 575394, 510711

SWEDEN – SUÈDE
Fritzes Information Center
Box 16356
Regeringsgatan 12
106 47 Stockholm   Tel. (08) 690.90.90
                              Telefax: (08) 20.50.21

Subscription Agency/Agence d'abonnements :
Wennergren-Williams Info AB
P.O. Box 1305
171 25 Solna   Tel. (08) 705.97.50
                              Téléfax : (08) 27.00.71

SWITZERLAND – SUISSE
Maditec S.A. (Books and Periodicals - Livres
et périodiques)
Chemin des Palettes 4
Case postale 266
1020 Renens   Tel. (021) 635.08.65
                              Telefax: (021) 635.07.80

Librairie Payot S.A.
4, place Pépinet
CP 3212
1002 Lausanne   Tel. (021) 341.33.48
                              Telefax: (021) 341.33.45

Librairie Unilivres
6, rue de Candolle
1205 Genève   Tel. (022) 320.26.23
                              Telefax: (022) 329.73.18

Subscription Agency/Agence d'abonnements :
Dynapresse Marketing S.A.
38 avenue Vibert
1227 Carouge   Tel.: (022) 308.07.89
                              Telefax : (022) 308.07.99

See also – Voir aussi :
OECD Publications and Information Centre
August-Bebel-Allee 6
D-53175 Bonn 2 (Germany) Tel. (0228) 959.120
                              Telefax: (0228) 959.12.17

TAIWAN – FORMOSE
Good Faith Worldwide Int'l. Co. Ltd.
9th Floor, No. 118, Sec. 2
Chung Hsiao E. Road
Taipei   Tel. (02) 391.7396/391.7397
                              Telefax: (02) 394.9176

THAILAND – THAÏLANDE
Suksit Siam Co. Ltd.
113, 115 Fuang Nakhon Rd.
Opp. Wat Rajbopith
Bangkok 10200   Tel. (662) 225.9531/2
                              Telefax: (662) 222.5188

TURKEY – TURQUIE
Kültür Yayinlari Is-Türk Ltd. Sti.
Atatürk Bulvari No. 191/Kat 13
Kavaklidere/Ankara   Tel. 428.11.40 Ext. 2458
Dolmabahce Cad. No. 29
Besiktas/Istanbul   Tel. 260.71.88
                              Telex: 43482B

UNITED KINGDOM – ROYAUME-UNI
HMSO
Gen. enquiries   Tel. (071) 873 0011
Postal orders only:
P.O. Box 276, London SW8 5DT
Personal Callers HMSO Bookshop
49 High Holborn, London WC1V 6HB
                              Telefax: (071) 873 8200
Branches at: Belfast, Birmingham, Bristol, Edin-
burgh, Manchester

UNITED STATES – ÉTATS-UNIS
OECD Publications and Information Centre
2001 L Street N.W., Suite 700
Washington, D.C. 20036-4910 Tel. (202) 785.6323
                              Telefax: (202) 785.0350

VENEZUELA
Libreria del Este
Avda F. Miranda 52, Aptdo. 60337
Edificio Galipán
Caracas 106   Tel. 951.1705/951.2307/951.1297
                          Telegram: Libreste Caracas

Subscription to OECD periodicals may also be
placed through main subscription agencies.

Les abonnements aux publications périodiques de
l'OCDE peuvent être souscrits auprès des
principales agences d'abonnement.

Orders and inquiries from countries where Distribu-
tors have not yet been appointed should be sent to:
OECD Publications Service, 2 rue André-Pascal,
75775 Paris Cedex 16, France.

Les commandes provenant de pays où l'OCDE n'a
pas encore désigné de distributeur devraient être
adressées à : OCDE, Service des Publications,
2, rue André-Pascal, 75775 Paris Cedex 16, France.

2-1994

PRINTED IN FRANCE

•

OECD PUBLICATIONS
2 rue André-Pascal
75775 PARIS CEDEX 16
No. 46975
(10 94 22 1) ISBN 92-64-14079-4
ISSN 0376-6438

•